IT'S MY PROPHET'S BIRTHDAY!

MAWLID AL-DĪBA'Ī
MADE EASY FOR KIDS

*Stories, Poems and Songs
in Praise of the Prophet Muhammad* ﷺ

COMPOSED BY
**SHAYKH `ABD AL-RAHMAN
IBN MUHAMMAD AL-DĪBA'Ī**

FOREWORD BY
SHAYKH MUHAMMAD NAZIM ADIL AL-HAQQANI

COMPILED BY
SHAYKH MUHAMMAD HISHAM KABBANI

ILLUSTRATIONS BY
**CHILDREN AND ARTISTS
FROM AROUND THE WORLD**

INSTITUTE FOR SPIRITUAL AND CULTURAL ADVANCEMENT

© Copyright 2023 Institute for Spiritual and Cultural Advancement. All rights reserved. No part of this book may be reproduced, stored in a retrieval system, or transmitted in any form, or by any means, electronic, mechanical, photocopying, or otherwise, without the written permission of ISCA.

ISBN: 978-1-938058-72-1

Printed in Istanbul, Turkey by Mega Basim.

For you, Yaa Rasoolullah...

Artwork by
Layka Sperling, 13,
Michigan, USA

Published and Distributed by:
INSTITUTE FOR SPIRITUAL
AND CULTURAL ADVANCEMENT
17195 Silver Parkway, #401
Fenton, MI 48430 USA
Tel: (888) 278-6624, Fax:(810) 815-0518

Email: staff@naqshbandi.org
Web: www.naqshbandi.org
Shop for other titles online at:
http://www.isn1.net

وَمَا أَرْسَلْنَاكَ إِلَّا رَحْمَةً لِّلْعَالَمِينَ

(O Muhammad!) We have not sent you except as A MERCY for all the worlds! (Surat al-Anbiya, 21:107)

قُلْ بِفَضْلِ ٱللَّهِ وَبِرَحْمَتِهِ فَبِذَٰلِكَ فَلْيَفْرَحُوا

Say: "In the Bounty of Allah, and in HIS MERCY, let them BE HAPPY!" (Surat Yunus, 10:58)

Artwork by Aisha Demartino-Bacon, 17, Michigan USA

MAWLID AN-NABI ﷺ MUBARAK!

CONTENTS

ACKNOWLEDGEMENTS — 7

FOREWORD — 9

INTRODUCTION — 11

1. THE OPENING — 15
    - AL-FATIHA — 17
2. THE OPENING QASIDAH — 19
3. ALLAH PRAISES HIS PROPHET — 21
4. HIS CREATION — 23
5. WHOM SHOULD WE RUN TO? — 29
6. HIS BLESSED DESCRIPTION — 33
7. THE CARAVANER'S QASIDAH — 39
8. TESTIMONY AND PRAISE — 41
9. HIS PURE ANCESTRY — 43
10. PREDICTION OF THE PROPHETIC KINGDOM — 44
11. MAWLID, HIS BIRTH — 47
12. YAA NABI SALAAM 'ALAYKA — 53
13. MARHABAN, MARHABAN — 55
14. RABBEE FAGHFIRLEE — 57
15. TALA'AL BADRU 'ALAYNA — 59
16. SALLALLAHU 'ALA MUHAMMAD — 61

17. QASIDA BURDAH	63
18. 'ALAL MADINAH	65
19. NAHRAN MIN LABAN	67
20. HIS YOUTH	69
21. DU'A, THE CLOSING PRAISE	91

THE COMPLETE QASIDAH LYRICS — 95

THE OPENING QASIDAH	96
THE CARAVANER'S QASIDAH	98
YAA NABI SALAAM 'ALAYKA	100
MARHABAN, MARHABAN	101
RABBEE FAGHFIRLEE	101
TALA'AL BADRU 'ALAYNA	102
SALLALLAHU 'ALA MUHAMMAD	102
QASIDAH BURDAH	103
'ALAL MADINAH	104
NAHRAN MIN LABAN	105

ACTIVITIES — 106

A TEST OF LOVE	106
THE ANSWERS	108
SIMPLE SUNNAHS, BIG REWARDS	110
LET'S FOLLOW HIS FOOTSTEPS!	111

Artwork by
artist Sana Mirza
Houstan, Texas, USA

ACKNOWLEDGEMENTS

We would like to extend our gratitude, first and foremost, to our Lord, Allah Almighty, for His Aid in the completion of this book. We also express our gratitude to His Beloved, our Prophet and Master Muhammad ﷺ, his Blessed Family and Companions, may Allah be pleased with them. To Allah we owe our worship and to His Beloved ﷺ, we owe our love and reverence.

We also wish to express our gratitude to the illustrious saints of the Naqshbandi Path, whose guidance continue to sustain us in our lives. We especially thank our teacher, Shaykh Muhammad Nazim al-Haqqani and Shaykh Muhammad Hisham Kabbani, may Allah sanctify their secrets and raise their stations, for their years of calling to Allah and His Beloved Messenger ﷺ with sincerity and love. We ask Allah to bless them and allow us to be with them in this life and the next.

Lastly, we would like to express our heartfelt appreciation to the children and their families, as well as the renowned artists from around the world, who contributed to this book with their beautiful illustrations.

Alice Skachkova, Moscow, Russia
Amir al-Zubi, Bosnia and Herzegovina
Doy Yuniarto Soewondo, Jakarta, Indonesia
Halime Karatas, Istanbul, Turkey
Hana Horack, Hedeper, Germany
Maliha Hashmi, Madinah, Saudi Arabia
Malika Ayubbi, Michigan, USA
Namra Khan, Delhi, India
Muna Hyunmin Bae, Incheon, Korea
Nurullaeva Mexriniso, Bukhara, Uzbekistan
Sana Mirza, Texas, USA
Yasmeen Olya, British Colombia, Canada
Aisha Demartino-Bacon (19), Michigan USA
Ameena Saleem (11), Texas, USA
Ayah Hussain (9), Rotterdam, The Netherlands
Beril Tunc (10), Golcuk, Turkiye
Fatima Bromund (21), Michigan, USA
Fatima (6) and Ahmad Magre (8), Tarim, Yemen
Gouwah Stevens (15), Cape Town, South Africa
Hassan Horack (23), Hedeper, Germany
Hussein Horack (23), Hedeper, Germany

Ibrahim (10) and Saira Hashmi, Massachusetts, USA
Kovsar Gurban (8), Baku, Azerbaijan
Layka Sperling (13), Michigan, USA
Mavisha (6) and Syeda Shoaib, Texas, USA
Menha (13) and Sadia Ahmad, New Jersey, USA
Meryem (17), Sarah (15) and Emine Tok (13)
   and Family, Michigan, USA
Muhammad Noor (9), Jamal al-Haqq (7)
   and Family, Ontario, Canada
Najia Horack (7), Hedeper, Germany
Nour (5) and Family, Vancouvar, Canada
NurJennah (9) and Siddique Family, Michigan, USA
Rana Z Dar (11), Maryland, USA
Rena Hasanli (10), Baku, Azerbaijan
Sabira Hasanli (11), Baku, Azerbaijan
Sarah Osier (19), Maryland, USA
Sounnia (7) and Alia Kabbani, Michigan, USA
Zaineb Tahir (16), Rawalpindi, Pakistan
Zahra Hussain (5) and Family, Michigan, USA
Zainab (23), Momina (22), Maryam (22)
   and Jamila Khan (17), Michigan, USA

We ask Allah, Subhanahu wa Ta`ala, to bless all of them and their loved ones, to gather them with the Prophet ﷺ, his Blessed family and Companions and to make their beautiful works a means for receiving the intercession of the Beloved ﷺ, in this life and next and that it be a source of his happiness and joy, inshaaAllah!

Portrait of As-Sayyid Shaykh Muhammad Nazim Adil al-Haqqani ق
by the late artist Yasmeen Olya, British Colombia, Canada,
commissioned for ISCA

FOREWORD

BY SHAYKH MUHAMMAD NAZIM ADIL AL-HAQQANI

Audhu billahi min ash-shaytaani 'r-rajeem,
Bismillahi 'r-Rahmani 'r-Raheem.

As-salamu `alaykum, O Servants of Allah! As-salamu `alaykum, O Believers! It is a holy month! It is Mawlid an-Nabi, Milad an-Nabi! Happy Birthday for the Seal of Prophets, Sayyidina Muhammad, sallAllahu `alayhi wa sallam!

Tonight all of Heavens are going to be decorated with such a decoration never seen before, for the glorifying of the joyous birth of the Seal of Prophets!

We are so happy to have reached the holiest month, Rabi'ul Awwal, in which Allah Almighty has sent His Most Beloved Servant, Sayyidina Muhammad, sallAllahu `alayhi wa sallam, to be a Mercy for all nations, as He said in the Holy Qur'an:

وَمَا أَرْسَلْنَاكَ إِلَّا رَحْمَةً لِّلْعَالَمِينَ

**(O Muhammad!) We have not sent you
except as a Mercy for all Creation!**
(Surat al-Anbiya, 21:107)

So, increase your salawat! Send much more praisings and blessings upon Sayyid al-Awwaleena wal Aakhireen, the Master of the First and Last Nations. Tonight, all angels and the souls of all Believers through Heavens are singing with such beautiful singing:

*Ya Muhammed, canim arzular seni!
Dost Muhammed, canim pek sever seni!*

**O Muhammad, my soul yearns for you!
O Friend Muhammad, my soul loves you dearly!**

Millions and billions that night will be in celebration in Heavens, as well as the real Believers on Earth, whose hearts are full with the love of Sayyidina Muhammad, sallAllahu `alayhi wa sallam!

Al-Fatihah.

INTRODUCTION

BY SHAYKH MUHAMMAD HISHAM KABBANI

Dear Children,

Know that the birth of our Prophet is the birth of Islam!
His light was the first to be created,
and from his light is the birth of all Creation!
He was and is still the Prophet of all prophets.
He is the Guiding Light of the Universe and Paradises!
He is the Ocean of Beauty and Majesty, the Sky of Happiness and Love.
He is the Perfect Servant of Allah! He is the Mirror of Allah's Reflections,
who brings the Light of Heavens on this dark earth.
He is the one who is with everyone, as Allah said:

"KNOW THAT THE PROPHET IS IN YOU!"
(Surah al-Hujurat, 49:7)

He is the one who will save humanity with his intercession!
He is the one who can stand in front of Allah, by Allah's Permission!
He is the Light, the One Dressed with Light upon Light!
His secrets are in the Heavens! His secrets are in Allah's Presence!
His secrets are like an abundant river! He is...

MUHAMMAD, THE MESSENGER OF ALLAH,
sallAllahu 'alayhi wa sallam!

He is the one who has been brought to Nearness,
a nearness angel Gabriel was unable to reach!
His level, no one can reach! His level, no angel, human or jinn can understand.
He is who he is, and only his Lord knows who he is!
He is the Jewel of Jewels, the Light of Lights, the Secret of Secrets,
The Heaven of Heavens, the Door to Allah's Presence, the Way to Every Seeker.
He is the one Allah sent as Mercy for Humanity. He is the Gifted Mercy!

So, O Human Beings! O Children! Be happy in His Mercy!
Allah gave him what He did not give anyone else!
Allah dressed him with what He did not dress anyone else!
Allah loved him with what He did not love anyone else!
He is Love! He is...

OUR MASTER MUHAMMAD,
sallAllahu 'alayhi wa sallam!

IF YOU WANT THE PROPHET, SALLALLAHU `ALAYHI WA SALLAM, TO ACCEPT YOU FROM AMONG HIS BLESSED FAMILY, THEN **LOVE** HIM! **LOVE** HIM AND SAY: "I **LOVE** YOU, YAA MUHAMMAD, YAA RASOOLALLAH, SALLALLAHU `ALAYHI WA SALLAM!"

WHEN YOU WAKE UP, SAY: "I LOVE YOU, YAA **MUHAMMAD**, SALLALLAHU `ALAYHI WA SALLAM!"

DURING THE DAY, SAY: "I LOVE YOU, YAA **MUHAMMAD**, SALLALLAHU `ALAYHI WA SALLAM!"

BEFORE YOU SLEEP, SAY: "I LOVE YOU, YAA **MUHAMMAD**, SALLALLAHU `ALAYHI WA SALLAM!"

Dear Children,

Before we begin the Mawlid, let us try something:
Close your eyes and open your hearts.
Imagine you are in Madinah, the City of Lights.
sitting in the presence of our Beloved Prophet,
sallAllahu `alayhi wa sallam.
Now place your hand on your heart
and put a smile on your face,
because the Best of Creation,
MUHAMMAD MUSTAFA,
sallAllahu `alayhi wa sallam,
is looking at you right now with a smile on his face,
a smile that lights up Heavens and Earth!
Now is the perfect time to say it,
to tell him how much you love him.
Go ahead! Say it loud and clear:
"I LOVE YOU, YAA RASOOLULLAH,
I LOVE YOU SO MUCH!"

Did you know that our Beloved Prophet,
sallAllahu `alayhi wa sallam,
always hears and responds to anyone
who calls on him and sends salawat,
peace and blessings, upon him?

And if you keep doing this small practice daily,
he may even show himself to you one day!

Say "YES!" if you want to see the Holy Prophet,
sallAllahu `alayhi wa sallam.

YES! YES! YES!

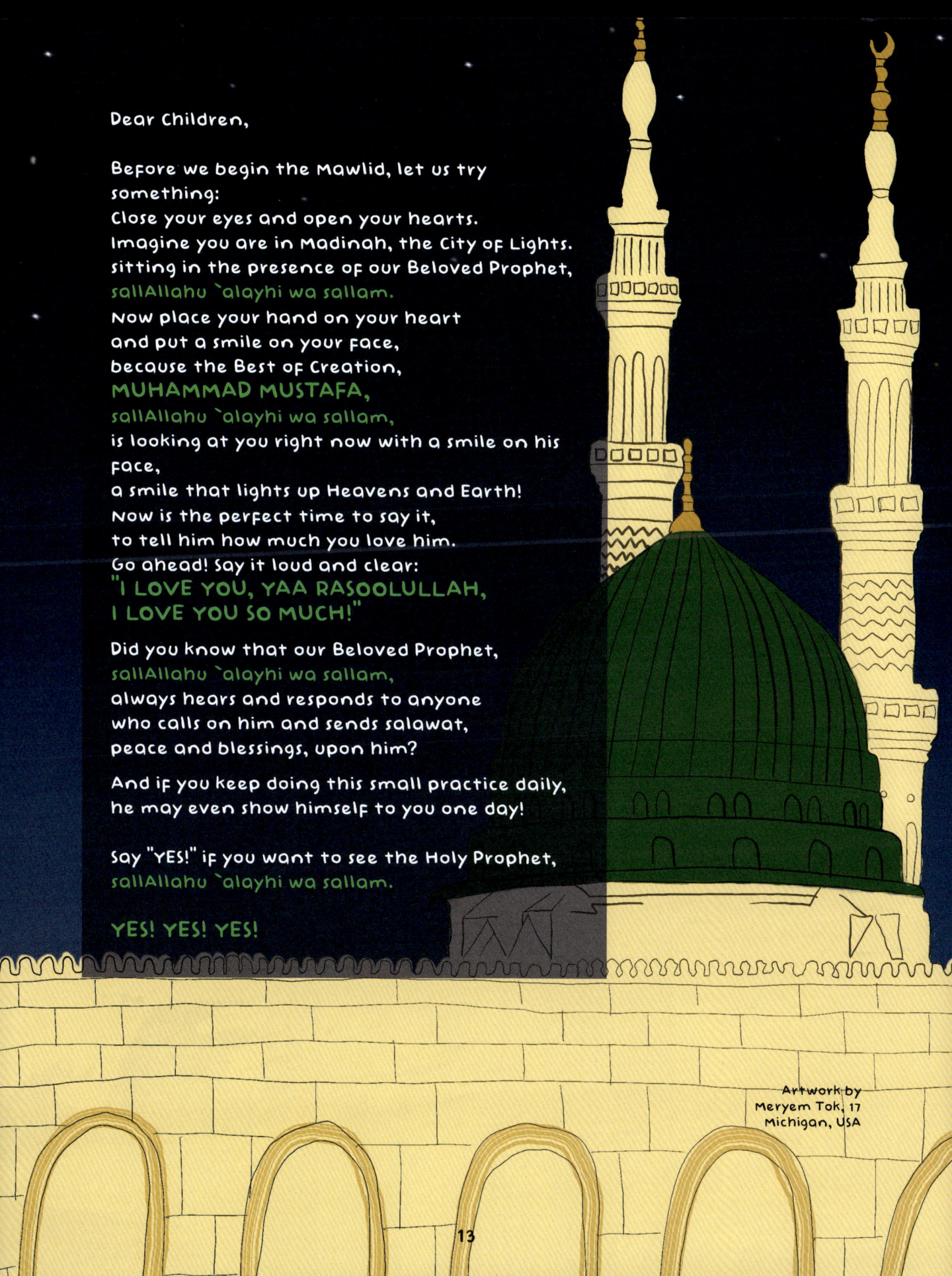

Artwork by
Meryem Tok, 17
Michigan, USA

Artwork by Nour, 5, and family, Vancouver, Canada

SAY AMEEN!

THE OPENING

بِسْمِ اللّٰهِ الرَّحْمٰنِ الرَّحِيمِ

Dear Children,
Let us all read the FATIHAH
for our benefit and yours,
for the benefit of our parents, our families,
and our shaykhs, our guiding lights,

for whoever is with us now and for whoever is absent,
for our living ones and our deceased ones,
for those who always come to these Mawlid gatherings,
and for whoever was a cause for our coming together today,
that Allah, The Most Generous,
fill our hearts with His Light,

Forgive our sins and bad manners,
protect us in the same way He protects His Qur'an,
and supports and gives us victory in the same way
He supported and gave victory to His prophets.
And may Allah, The Most Generous,
shower this gathering in goodness, in happiness,
in lights and in blessings,

and may He take care of all our needs
for the sake of the Best of All Creation,
Sayyidina Muhammad, Peace and Blessings be upon him!

Illustration of Shaykh Muhammad Nazim Adil al-Haqqani (right) with his son-in-law, Shaykh Muhammad Hisham Kabbani (middle), and his brother, Shaykh Muhammad Adnan Kabbani (left), by artist, Halime Karatas, Istanbul, Turkey

أَعُوذُ بِاللهِ مِنَ الشَّيْطَانِ الرَّجِيمِ

بِسْمِ اللهِ الرَّحْمٰنِ الرَّحِيمِ ﴿١﴾ اَلْحَمْدُ لِلّٰهِ رَبِّ الْعَالَمِينَ ﴿٢﴾ اَلرَّحْمٰنِ الرَّحِيمِ ﴿٣﴾ مَالِكِ يَوْمِ الدِّينِ ﴿٤﴾ اِيَّاكَ نَعْبُدُ وَاِيَّاكَ نَسْتَعِينُ ﴿٥﴾ اِهْدِنَا الصِّرَاطَ الْمُسْتَقِيمَ ﴿٦﴾ صِرَاطَ الَّذِينَ اَنْعَمْتَ عَلَيْهِمْ غَيْرِ الْمَغْضُوبِ عَلَيْهِمْ وَلَا الضَّالِّينَ ﴿٧﴾

1. Bismillaahir-Rahmaanir-Raheem
2. Alhamdulillaahi rabbil `alameen
3. Ar-rahmaanir-raheem
4. Maaliki yawmiddeen
5. Iyyaaka na`budu wa iyyaaka nasta`een
6. Ihdinas siraat al-mustaqeem
7. Siraat alladheena an`amta `alayhim ghayril maghdubi `alayhim wa laddaalleen.
Ameen!

1. In the name of Allah, Most Gracious, Most Merciful.
2. Praise be to Allah, Lord of the Worlds,
3. Most Gracious, Most Merciful
4. Master of the Day of Judgment
5. It is You we worship and You we ask for help
6. Guide us to the Straight Path
7. The path of those upon whom You have bestowed favor, not of those who have earned Your anger or of those who are astray.
Ameen!

Surat al-Fatihah, 1:7

Drawing of
"Baab us-Salaam"
by Hussein Horack, 23
Hedeper, Germany

THE OPENING QASIDAH

(Recite 2 times or more)

يَا رَبِّ صَلِّ عَلَى مُحَمَّد

يَا رَبِّ صَلِّ عَلَيْهِ وَسَلِّمْ

Yaa Rabbi salli `alaa Muhammad
O Lord, bestow blessings upon Muhammad.

Yaa Rabbi salli `alayhi wa sallim
O Lord, bestow blessings and peace be upon him.

Allahumma salli wa sallim wa barik `alayhi wa `ala aalih.
O Allah! Exalt, bless and send peace on him and his family.

Artwork by
Aisha Demartino-Bacon, 19
Michigan, USA

ALLAH PRAISES HIS PROPHET

أَعُوذُ بِاللهِ مِنَ الشَّيْطَانِ الرَّجِيمِ
بِسْمِ اللهِ الرَّحْمٰنِ الرَّحِيمِ

A`oodhu billaahi mina'sh-shaytaani 'r-rajeem.
Bismillaahi 'r-Rahmaani 'r-Raheem.
I seek the protection of Allah from the accursed Satan.
In the name of God, the Beneficent, the Merciful.

إِنَّ اللَّهَ وَمَلَائِكَتَهُ يُصَلُّونَ عَلَى النَّبِيِّ

يَا أَيُّهَا الَّذِينَ آمَنُوا صَلُّوا عَلَيْهِ وَسَلِّمُوا تَسْلِيمًا

InnaLlaaha wa malaa'ikatahu yusalloona `alan Nabiyy. Yaa ayyuhal-ladheena aamanoo salloo `alayhi wa sallimoo tasleemaa.

Allah and His Angels send blessings on the Prophet. O you who believe! Send blessings on him, and salute him with all respect. (Surah al-Ahzab, 33:56)

> Allahumma salli wa sallim wa barik `alayhi wa `ala aalih.
> O Allah! Exalt, bless and send peace on him and his family.

Artwork by
Sarah Osier, 20
Maryland, USA

TIME TO LISTEN

HIS CREATION

> Allahumma salli wa sallim wa barik `alayhi wa `ala aalih.
> O Allah! Exalt, bless and send peace on him and his family.

All praise be to Allah, who is Strong and Powerful. He is the Protecting Friend, the Giver of Blessings and Remover of all our sadness. He is the Knower of all beings. All the stars sing His Priases. All of Creation declare His Oneness, saying:

LAA ILAHA ILLALLAH,
There is no God but Allah!

He is The Wise One whose Wisdom manifest in the wonders of His creations. He created the brain, bones, the upper arms, the veins, the flesh, the skin, the hair and the blood in a poetic harmonious arrangement.

LAA ILAHA ILLALLAH,
There is no God but Allah!

Artwork by
Kovsar Gurban, 8
Baku, Azerbaijan

He is The Generous One who spreads over His Creation a carpet of generosity and worldly talent and provisions, descending every night to the lower Heaven, calling out:

"Is there anyone asking for forgiveness so that he may be forgiven?"

TAA'IBOONA ILALLAAH,
We seek repentance to Allah!

"Is there anyone asking for a favor so that his request may be granted?"

If only you saw those who serve standing on their feet or sitting on their knees, their tears pouring before their Lord, fearing for themselves, and they run from their sins towards Allah. For they are the ones who continuously seek forgiveness until the light of dawn. And they returned successfully having achieved their aims with the blessings of Allah's Beloved, until not one man amongst them returned in despair.

LAA ILAHA ILLALLAH,
There is no God but Allah!

Then Allah, Subhaanahu wa Ta`aala, presented the Pride of His creation and said: "This is the leader amongst all the prophets, the most honored of the pure ones and the most honored amongst those I love!"

Artwork by artist Sana Mirza, Houston, Texas, USA

TIME TO LISTEN

WHOM SHOULD WE RUN TO?

> Allahumma salli wa sallim wa barik `alayhi wa `ala aalih.
> O Allah! Exalt, bless and send peace on him and his family.

After Allah showed the Light of Muhammad,
sallAllahu `alayhi wa sallam,
to His Angels in Heaven, the angels asked:

"Is that the Light of Adam,
`alayhi 's-salaam?"
Allah said: "Because of this light,
I gave Adam a high status!"

The angels asked: "Is it Nuh,
`alayhis '-salaam?"
Allah said: "Because of him,
Nuh and all his family and friends
were safe from drowning in his ark!"

The angels asked: "Is it Ibrahim, *`alayhi 's-salaam*?"
Allah said: "Because of him (Muhammad), Ibrahim was able to make his case against the worshipping of idols and stars."

The angels asked: "Is it Musa, *`alayhi 's-salaam*?"
Allah said: "Musa is his brother, but he is Allah's Beloved, while Moses only spoke with Him."

The angels asked: "Is it `Isa, *`alayhi 's-salaam*?"
Allah said: "`Isa only brought the good news of his prophethood. `Isa is only the guard in front of the palace of his prophethood."

The angels asked: "So who is this person, this Beloved one upon whom You granted the Supreme Crown?"

Allah, *Subhaanahu wa Ta`ala*, said:
"He is the Prophet that I have chosen from the descendants of Lu'ayy ibn Ghaalib.
His father and mother passed away. He was looked after by his grandfather, then by his uncle Abu Talib."

Artwork by
Jamila Khan, 17
Michigan, USA

Artwork by
Muhammad Noor, 9
Jamal al-Haqq Masood, 7
and Family, Ontario, Canada

TIME TO LISTEN

HIS BLESSED DESCRIPTION

> Allahumma salli wa sallim wa barik `alayhi wa `ala aalih.
> O Allah! Exalt, bless and send peace on him and his family.

He was raised among the People of Tihama,
close to the Day of Reckoning.

On his back is a mark.

He was shaded by the clouds wherever he went
and the rain clouds obeyed his command.

His forehead shone like the morning;
his hair dark like the night.

Alfiyyul-anfi, meemiyyul-fami, nooniyyul-haajib. His nose was like the letter Alif, his mouth like the letter Meem, and his eyebrows like the letter Noon.

Sam`uhu yasma`u sareeral-qalami, basaruhu ilas-sab`it tibaaqi thaaqib. His hearing heard the scratching of the Pen; his sight could penetrate the seven skies!

Artwork by artist,
Hana Horack
Hedeper, Germany

Artwork by
Ameena Saleem, 11
Texas, USA

The camel kissed his two feet, after which all its suffering from overburdening and abuse was relieved.

The lizard asserted its faith in him and even the mimosa trees saluted him. Stones spoke to him. The stump of the date tree longed for him with a sad and lamenting yearning.

His two hands would manifest their blessings
in the increase of food and drink.
His heart was never unmindful and never slept,
but rather stood ready for His Lord's duty and service.
If he was harmed, he forgave and never took revenge.
When affronted, he kept silent and did not respond.

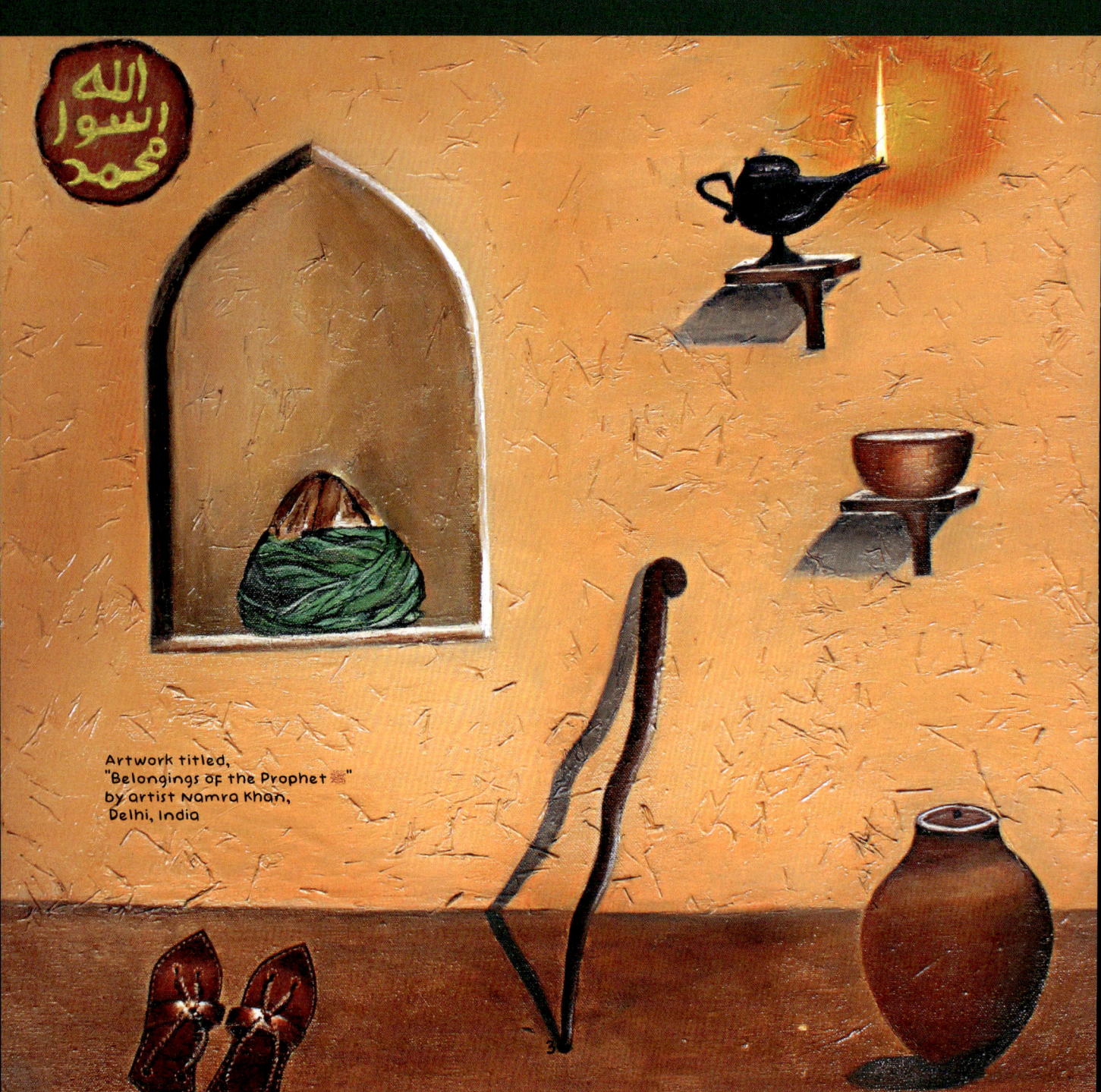

Artwork titled,
"Belongings of the Prophet ﷺ"
by artist Namra Khan,
Delhi, India

Artwork by
Ayah Hussein, 9
Rotterdam, The Netherlands

(Allah said:) I raised him to the highest of degrees on a mount that is not fit for anyone before or after him, in a gathering of angels that exceeds all gatherings, until he rose above the Station of the Two Universes, arriving within two bows' lengths of the Divine Presence. During this time I was the Companion with whom he spoke. I returned him from the Station of the Throne, before his bed became cold, and after he received what he desired.

> Remember, when the soil of Taybah was honored to bear his form. Then there raced to him the souls of everyone who loved him, some on foot and others upon camels!

Artwork by
Kovsar Gurban, 8
Baku, Azerbaijan

THE CARAVANER'S QASIDAH

(Recite 2 times or more)

صَلَاةُ اللهِ مَا لَاحَتْ كَوَاكِبْ

عَلَى أَحْمَدْ خَيْرِ مَنْ رَكِبَ النَّجَائِبْ

SalaatuLlaahi maa laahat kawaakib
Allah's blessings appear as many as the stars in the sky.

`Ala 'hmad khayri man rakiban-najaa'ib
Upon Ahmad, the best of those who ride the camels.

Allahumma salli wa sallim wa barik `alayhi wa `ala aalih.
O Allah! Exalt, bless and send peace on him and his family.

무함마드 으르라 을라히 일라 라

The Islamic Testimony of Faith calligraphed in Korean calligraphy with Arabic 'nuqtas' (dots). This is a piece representing Korean Muslims through cultural and religious objects.

Artwork titled "Testimony" by Korean artist, Muna Hyunmin Bae, Incheon, Korea

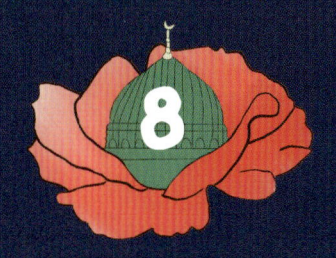

TESTIMONY AND PRAISE

Glory be to He who dignified the Holy Prophet, sallAllahu `alayhi wa sallam, with the most honorable origin and status. I praise him for all he received from Allah's bountiful grants.

I bear witness that there is no God but Allah,
the One and Only, without partner,
LORD OF THE EASTS AND THE WESTS.
And I bear witness that our leader Muhammad
is His Servant and Messenger
SENT TO ALL MANKIND,
BOTH THE NON-ARABS
AND THE ARABS!

May Allah's blessings and salutations be upon him and his Family and Companions, owners of gloriously remembered deeds and history. Unending obligatory Blessings and Salutations! Who utters them will not be disappointed when they come before him on the Day of Rising!

> Allahumma salli wa sallim wa barik `alayhi wa `ala aalih.
> O Allah! Exalt, bless and send peace on him and his family.

TIME TO LISTEN

Artwork by Najia Horack, 14
Hedeper, Germany

9

HIS PURE ANCESTRY

As related by `Abd Allah ibn Abbas, the Messenger of Allah said in a hadith, "Verily, the Quraysh was a light chosen by Allah before He created Adam by two thousand years. The Light of Muhammad glorified Allah, and the angels also glorified Allah following it. When Allah created Adam, He placed this light in his clay. So Allah sent down my light to the face of the earth in the loins of Adam, and it was carried in the loins of Noah when he was on the ark. And He put me in the loins of Abraham when he was thrown in the fire. That was how Allah moved me from noble loins and pure wombs, until He brought me out from between my two parents, and none of them ever committed fornication, whatsoever!"

Allahumma salli wa sallim wa barik `alayhi wa `ala aalih.
O Allah! Exalt, bless and send peace on him and his family.

10

PREDICTION OF THE PROPHETIC KINGDOM

One of the Companions of the Prophet, sallAllahu 'alayhi wa sallam, Ka`ab al-Ahbar, once said:

"(Before accepting Islam) My father taught me the whole Torah, except one section which he kept sealed and hidden in a safe box. When my father passed away I opened it and it read:

There will come a Messenger at the end of time, his birth is in Mecca, he emigrates to Madinah and his kingship will be in Damascus. He cuts his hair and wears a waist-cloth. He is the best amongst the prophets, and his followers are the best amongst people.

They glorify Allah with every honor bestowed on them. They keep straight rows during their prayers just as they do in battle. Their hearts are enscribed (with Allah's Book) and they thank Allah in every condition whether in difficulty or ease.

Artwork by Beril Tunc, 10, Golcuk, Turkiye

A third of his people will enter Heaven without their deeds being weighed!

Allahummaj`alnaa minhum,
O Allah, make us from among them!

A third will come with sins and mistakes, but they will be forgiven.
And a third will come bearing heavy sins and grave mistakes.

So Allah will order the Angels: "O My Angels! Go and weigh their deeds!"

The angels will say: "O our Lord, we find that these people oppressed
themselves and their sinful deeds are like mountains,
except for their bearing witness that there is no god but Allah
and Muhammad is the Messenger of Allah:

Ashhadu an laa ilaaha illaLlaah
wa ashhadu anna Muhammadan Rasoolullah.
I bear witness that there is no god but Allah
and I bear witness that Muhammad is the Messenger of Allah.

So Allah Almighty will say: "By My Honor and My Majesty, I will not make equal
those who are sincere to Me by their witnessing My Oneness like those who
belied Me. Let them enter the Garden of Paradise by My Mercy!"

Artwork by
artist Doy Yuniarto Soewondo,
Jakarta, Indonesia

MAWLID, HIS BIRTH

Listen with your hearts, O Children of Light, while I read you the beautiful qualities of the Most Beloved One, who received the greatest gifts from his Lord and saw the Beauty of Allah, Subhaanahu wa Ta`ala, with no veil!

When the time arrived for the dawn of the sun of prophethood in the sky of majesty, Allah, Subhaanahu wa Ta`ala, said to Angel Gabriel:

"O Gabriel! Announce the good news to all of Creation, with My congratulations and good tidings. The Chosen Light and Secret of Existence, which I created before the existence of all things and before the creation of Heavens and Earth...

Allahumma salli wa sallim wa barik `alayhi wa `ala aalih.
O Allah! Exalt, bless and send peace on him and his family.

On this night I move the light
of My Beloved Muhammad,
sallAllahu `alayhi wa sallam,
to the womb of his mother happy!

I fill this world
with his light!
I help him
in his childhood
as an orphan,
and I purify him
and his Family
with the highest
purification!"

Artwork by the late artist,
Yasmeen Olya (rahimahullah)
British Colombia, Canada

"أَمْلَأْ بِهِ الكَوْنَ نُورًا"

"& Fill This World With his Light"

So, the Throne shook with happiness and delight. And the Footstool increased in magnificence and greatness.

Allahumma salli wa sallim wa barik `alayhi wa `ala aalih.
O Allah! Exalt, bless and send peace on him and his family.

Artwork by
Menha Ahmad, 13, and Sadia Ahmad,
New Jersey, USA

The sky was filled with a brilliant light, and the voices of the angels vibrating with the recitation of God's Oneness, praising Him and seeking His forgiveness:

SubhaanAllah wal-hamduliLlah wa laa ilaaha illaLlah waLlaahu Akbar!

(Recite 4 times)

So, his mother continued to experience many signs of his eminence and honor until the completion of her pregnancy.

When the labor pains strengthened, with the permission of Allah, the Creator of All Creations, his mother gave birth...

...to the Beloved Prophet, sall-Allahu `alayhi wa sallam, in prostration, thanking and praising Allah as if he were the full moon in its splendor!

Artwork by artist Malika Ayubbi, Michigan, USA

Artwork by
Zahra Hussain, 5
and family,
Michigan, USA

YAA NABI SALAAM 'ALAYKA

(Recite 2 times or more)

يَا نَبِي سَلامْ عَلَيْكَ

يَا رَسُولْ سَلامْ عَلَيْكَ

يَا حَبِيبْ سَلامْ عَلَيْكَ

صَلَوَاتُ اللهِ عَلَيْكَ

Yaa Nabee salaam `alayka
Yaa Rasool salaam `alayka

O Prophet! Peace be upon you!
O Messenger! Peace be upon you!

Yaa Habeeb salaam `alayka
Salawaatullah `alayka

O Beloved! Peace be upon you!
Praises of Allah be upon you!

مرحبا

Artwork by
Zainab Khan, 23
Michigan, USA

MARHABAN, MARHABAN

(Recite 2 times or more)

مَرْحَبًا مَرْحَبًا يَا نُوْرَ عَيْنِي

مَرْحَبًا مَرْحَبًا جَدَّ الْحُسَيْنِ

Marhaban Marhaban
yaa noora `aynee

Greetings! Greetings!
O the light of my eyes!

Marhaban Marhaban
jaddal-Husayni

Greetings! Greetings!
O Grandfather of al-Husayn!

Artwork by
Gouwah Stevens, 15
Cape Town, South Africa

RABBEE FAGHFIRLEE

(Recite 2 times or more)

رَبِّ فَاغْفِرْ لِيْ ذُنُوْبِيْ يَا اللّٰه

بِبَرَكَةِ الْهَادِيْ مُحَمَّدْ يَا اللّٰه

Rabbi faghfir lee dhunoobee yaa Allah

O my Lord, forgive me,
for I have sins, O Allah!

Bi barakaatil haadee Muhammad yaa Allah

With the blessings of my guide Muhammad, O Allah!

Artwork by
NurJennah Siddique, 9
and Family
Michigan, USA

TALA'AL BADRU 'ALAYNA

(Recite 2 times or more)

طَلَعَ الْبَدْرُ عَلَينَا

مِنْ ثَنِيَّاتِ الْوَدَاعِ

وَجَبَ الشُّكْرُ عَلَينَا

مَا دَعَا لِلَّهِ دَاعٍ

Tala`al badru `alaynaa
min thaneeyyaatil wadaa`a

The full moon rose above us
From the valley of wadaa`a

Wajabash shukru `alaynaa
maa da`aalillaahee daa`a

Gratitude is our obligation
as long as any caller calls to Allah.

Artwork by
Momina Khan, 22
Michigan, USA

SALLALLAHU 'ALA MUHAMMAD

(Recite 2 times or more)

صَلَّى اللهُ عَلَى مُحَمَّدْ

صَلَّى اللهُ عَلَيهِ وَسَلَّمْ

Sall-Allaahu `alaa Muhammad
May Allah send prayers upon Muhammad!

Sall-Allaahu `alayhi wa sallam
May Allah send prayers and peace upon him!

Allahumma salli wa sallim wa barik `alayhi wa `ala aalih.
O Allah! Exalt, bless and send peace on him and his family.

فَمَبلَغُ العِلمِ فيهِ أنَّهُ بَشَرٌ
وَ أنَّهُ خَيرُ خَلقِ اللهِ كُلِّهِم

"The most we know of him is that he is a human being, and yet he is the best of all of Allah's creation!"

Imam Busayri

Artwork by
Sarah Tok, 15
and Meryem Tok, 17
Michigan, USA

QASIDAH BURDAH

(Recite 2 times or more)

يَا رَبِّ بِالْمُصْطَفَى بَلِّغْ مَقَاصِدَنَا

وَاغْفِرْ لَنَا مَا مَضَى يَا وَاسِعَ الْكَرَمِ

Yaa Rabbi bil-Mustaafaa balligh maqaasidanaa

O my Lord! By means of the Chosen One let us achieve our goals.

waghfir lanaa maa madaa yaa waasi`al-karami

And forgive our past misdeeds, O Possessor of Vast Generosity!

Allahumma salli wa sallim wa barik `alayhi wa `ala aalih.
O Allah! Exalt, bless and send peace on him and his family.

Artwork by
Maryam Khan, 22
Michigan, USA

'ALAL-MADINAH

(Recite 2 times or more)

عَلَى الْمَدِينَةْ عَلَى الْمَدِينَةْ

رَبِّ بَلِّغْنَا زِيَارَةْ نَبِينَا

رَبِّ بَلِّغْنَا نَزُورُ الْحَضْرَةْ

وَنُشَاهِدْ آحْمَدْ وَالْقُبَّةَ الْخَضْرَا

`Alal-Madeenah, `alal-Madeenah
To Madinah, onwards to Madinah!

Rabbi ballighnaa ziyaarat Nabeena
My Lord, grant us a visit to our Prophet! (Ameen.)

Rabbi ballighnaa nazoorul-hadrah
My Lord, grant us to visit the living one

wan-shaahid Ahmad wal-qubbal-khadrah
to witness Ahmad and the Green Dome! (Ameen.)

Allahumma salli wa sallim wa barik `alayhi wa `ala aalih.
O Allah! Exalt, bless and send peace on him and his family.

Artwork by
Fatimah Bromund, 21
Michigan, USA

NAHRAN MIN LABAN

(Recite 2 times or more)

إِنَّ فِي الْجَنَّةِ نَهْرًا مِنْ لَبَنْ

لِعَلِيٍّ وَحُسَيْنٍ وَحَسَنْ

Inna fil-jannati nahraan min laban
In Heaven there is a river of milk.

li 'Allyyin wa Husaynin wa Hasan
For Ali and Husayn and Hasan.

Allahumma salli wa sallim wa barik `alayhi wa `ala aalih.
O Allah! Exalt, bless and send peace on him and his family.

Artwork by artist
Nurullaeva Mexriniso at
Bukhara, Uzbekistan

20

HIS YOUTH

> *Allahumma salli wa sallim wa barik `alayhi wa `ala aalih.*
> O Allah! Exalt, bless and send peace on him and his family.

When the Prophet, *sallAllahu `alayhi wa sallam*, was born,
his light rose from the desert of Arabia,
filling and shining the whole universe.
All of Heavens and Earth sparkled from his light!

Many miraculous events took place at the time of his birth.
The first miracle was the Persian fire, which had been
burning for a thousand years, went out.
Fourteen towers of the Palace of Kisra fell down.
And the devils of the sky were hit by shooting stars.

His radiant presence rose from the creation of his light,
and his beautiful light shone brilliantly until he was
presented to his nurse-mother.

The Quraysh asked:
"Who is going to support and look after this precious orphan who is so priceless in value?"

All the birds said:
"We will support him! We will support him!"

The wild beasts said:
"No, we have the first rights
and are more suited to support him,
so that we may receive his honor and grandeur!"

Then it was said:
"O company of nations, calm down!
Allah, with His wisdom, has determined that
the Prophet Muhammad,
sallAllahu `alayhi wa sallam, will have
Halima 'the tender-hearted' as his nurse-mother!"

As it happened, all turned away from
nursing him, as was previously written
in the Hidden Divine Plan unfolded such that
Halima binti Abu Dhu'ayb's good fortune
was to become his wet-nurse.

Artwork by artist Hana Horack
Hedeper, Germany

When Halima's gaze fell upon him, sallAllahu `alayhi wa sallam, she quickly placed him on her lap and cuddle him to her chest. A smile appeared on his face for her, as a light shone from his mouth and rose to the sky.

Artwork by
Emine Tok, 13
Michigan, USA

Artwork by
Ibrahim Hashmi, 10
and Saira Hashmi
Massachusetts, USA

She then took him under her care and went back to her family. When they arrived at her village, she saw the blessings he brought with him even affect her sheep. Then, every day she noticed the signs of greatness, as his station continued to increase, always in the custody of Allah, Subhaanahu wa Ta`ala's gentleness and safeguard. Then, he grew up and mixed with his foster siblings and other children.

One day, when the Beloved Prophet, *sallAllahu `alayhi wa sallam*, was away from his homeland, there appeared three persons, their faces shining like the moon and the sun.

The other children ran away, while the Prophet, *sallAllahu `alayhi wa sallam*, stood by in amazement. Then they laid him on the ground gently and cut open his chest with a delicate incision. They took out the heart of "The Master of the Children of Adnan", cut it open with the knife of charity, removed from him the share belonging to shaytan, and filled it up with patience, knowledge, faith, certainty and contentment, and then returned him to his original place. The Beloved, *sallAllahu `alayhi wa sallam*, was standing again where he was previously.

Then said the angels:
"O the Beloved of the Most Merciful Lord!
If you knew what was planned for you of goodness, then you would have known your status compared to others and that would have increased you in joy and happiness.

Artwork by
Rana Z Dar, 11
Maryland, USA

O Muhammad! Rejoice!

Your knowledge was spread throughout all creations, and all creatures rejoice at your arrival. There will not be a single one of Allah's creations except that it comes to acknowledge your leadership, obey your orders, and listen to your speech.

Artwork by
Sounnia Kabbani, 7
Michigan, USA

And the camel will come to you,
asking for your help and protection.
The lizard and the gazelle will both bear
witness to your prophethood.
The trees, the moon and the wolves will soon
announce your prophethood.
And the Buraq which will be your mount,
longs to see your beauty!

بسم الله الرحمن الرحيم

"Archangel Gabriel has spoken of you across all horizons. The moon will be ordered to split for you. Every being in the universe was waiting and longing for your appearance. Their expectations were to see your shining light!"

While the Beloved, sallAllahu `alayhi wa sallam, was quietly listening to their voices, his smiling face was beaming like the morning light.

Artwork by
Sounnia Kabbani, 7
and Alia Kabbani
Michigan, USA

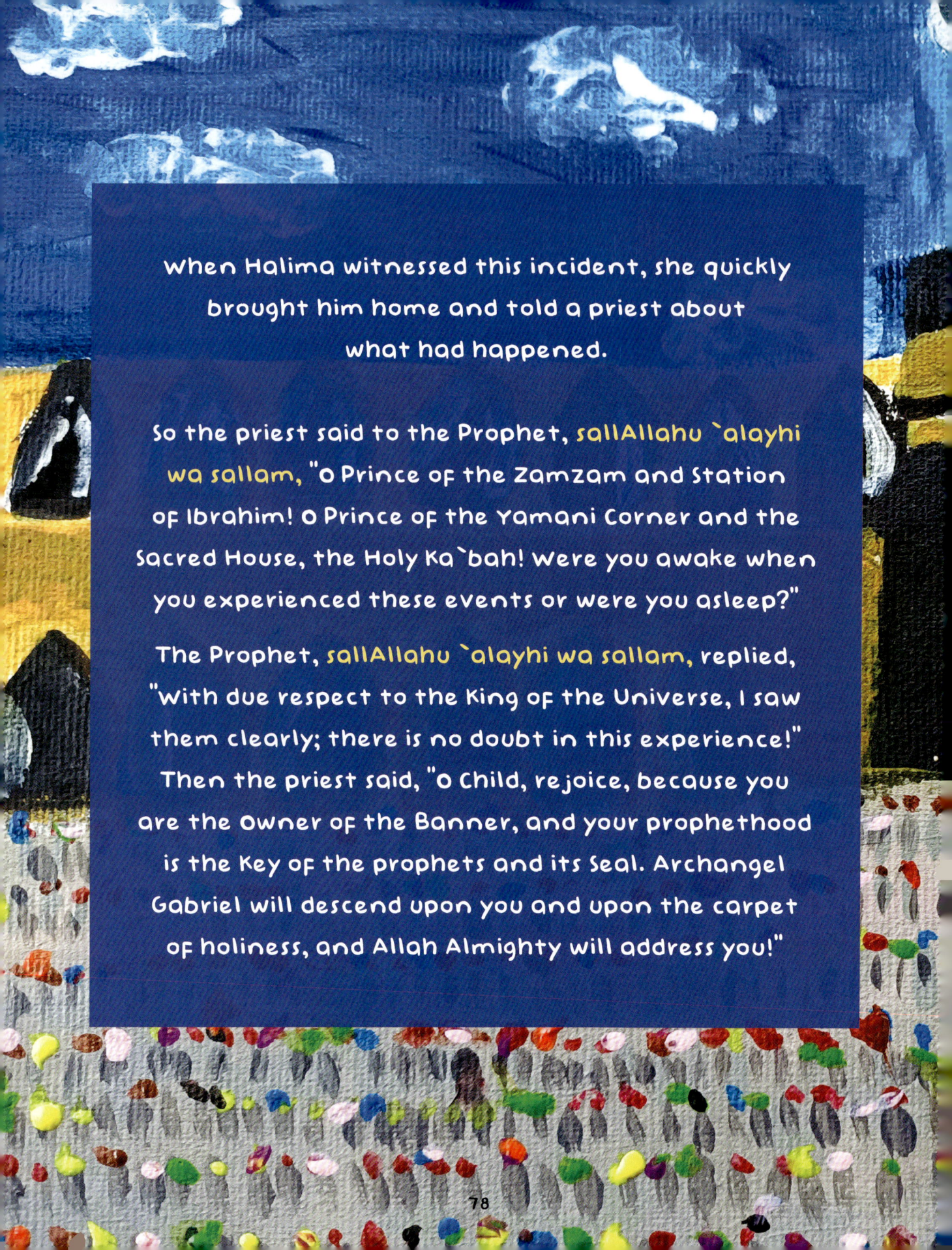

When Halima witnessed this incident, she quickly brought him home and told a priest about what had happened.

So the priest said to the Prophet, sallAllahu `alayhi wa sallam, "O Prince of the Zamzam and Station of Ibrahim! O Prince of the Yamani Corner and the Sacred House, the Holy Ka`bah! Were you awake when you experienced these events or were you asleep?"

The Prophet, sallAllahu `alayhi wa sallam, replied, "With due respect to the King of the Universe, I saw them clearly; there is no doubt in this experience!" Then the priest said, "O Child, rejoice, because you are the Owner of the Banner, and your prophethood is the Key of the prophets and its Seal. Archangel Gabriel will descend upon you and upon the carpet of holiness, and Allah Almighty will address you!"

Artwork by
Ayah Hussein, 9
Rotterdam,
The Netherlands

وَ إِنَّكَ لَعَلَى خُلُقٍ عَظِيمٍ

Artwork by
Fatima Magre, 6
and Ahmad Magre, 8
Tarim, Yemen

وَإِنَّكَ لَعَلَىٰ خُلُقٍ عَظِيمٍ

(O Muhammad!)
Indeed, you are of the most exalted character.
(Surat al-Qalam, 68:4)

Let it be known that Allah's Messenger, sallAllahu `alayhi wa sallam, is the Best of Mankind, physically and in character, the most righteous in his guidance to the path of truth:

- His morals were that of the Holy Qur'an.
- Giving sincere advice, doing good deeds, and forgiving others was his habit.
- Whoever saw him, respected him by instinct.
- When the poor called upon him, he always responded.
- The Prophet, sallAllahu `alayhi wa sallam, spoke the absolute truth and he never hid anything from the Muslims, nor cheated nor harmed.
- Whoever saw his holy face recognized that his was not the face of a liar.
- God's Messenger, sallAllahu `alayhi wa sallam, never criticized or shamed others.

Artwork by
Mavisha Shoaib, 6
and Syeda Shoaib
Texas, USA

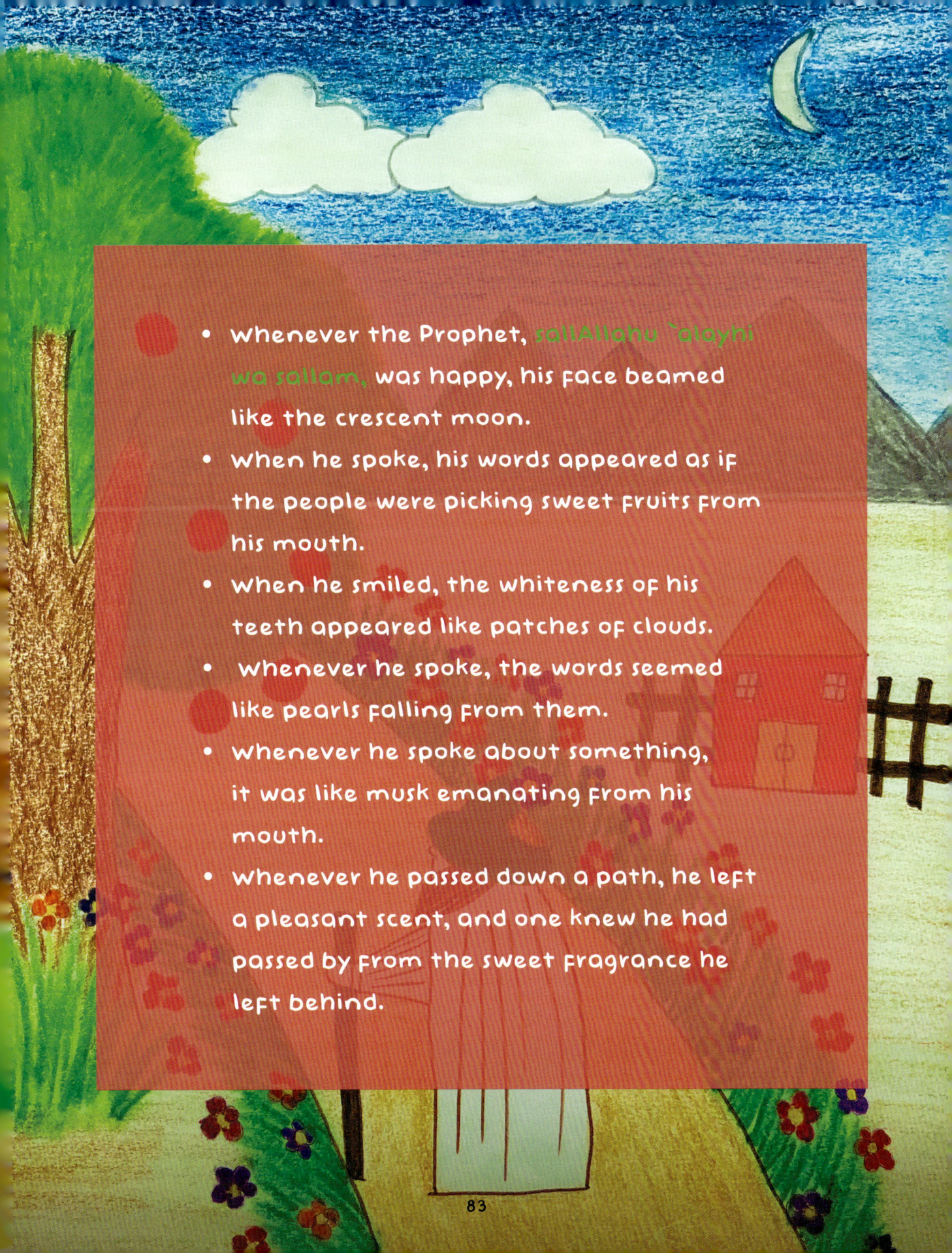

- Whenever the Prophet, sallAllahu `alayhi wa sallam, was happy, his face beamed like the crescent moon.
- When he spoke, his words appeared as if the people were picking sweet fruits from his mouth.
- When he smiled, the whiteness of his teeth appeared like patches of clouds.
- Whenever he spoke, the words seemed like pearls falling from them.
- Whenever he spoke about something, it was like musk emanating from his mouth.
- Whenever he passed down a path, he left a pleasant scent, and one knew he had passed by from the sweet fragrance he left behind.

- God's Messenger, sallAllahu `alayhi wa sallam, was more generous with his wealth than the blowing wind and he treated with kindness the orphans and widows.
- Whenever he sat in a congregation, his scent lingered for days. The best fragrance came from him, though he had not used perfume.
- If he walked amongst his companions, it is as if the moon were surrounded by a bouquet of stars. At night, the people felt as if it were noon due to his light.

Artwork by artist,
Doy Yuniarto Soewondo,
Jakarta, Indonesia

- Some companions said, "I have not seen anyone more attractive with black turban and red cloak than he, Allah's Messenger, sallAllahu `alayhi wa sallam."
- It had been said, "His face was brighter than the moon in a clear sky!"
- One of those who described him, said, "I have never seen anyone like him, before him or after him."
- Even the most eloquent tongue fails in trying to encompass his excellence.

Artwork by Hassan Horack, 23
Hedeper, Germany

Artwork by
Jamila Khan, 17
Michigan, USA

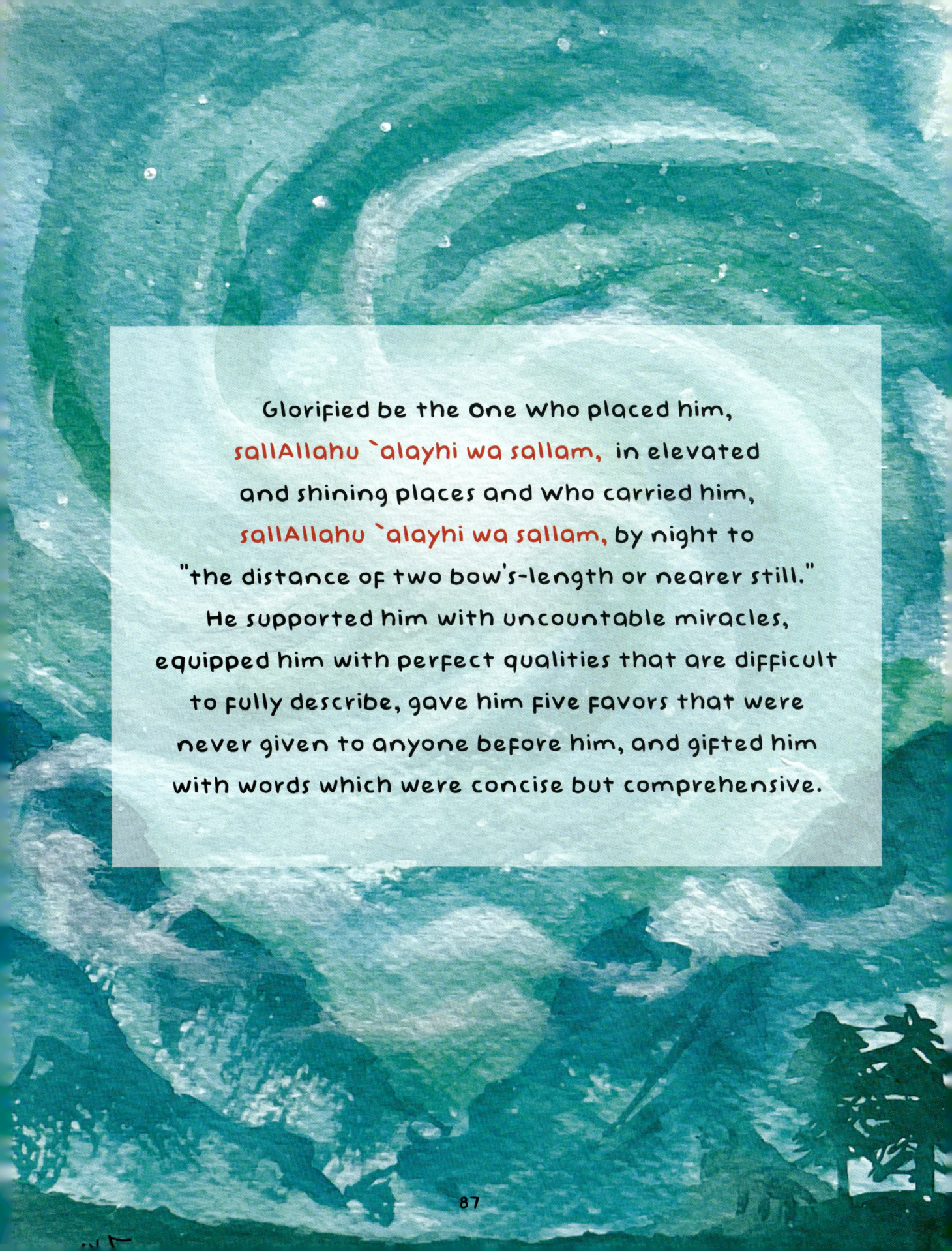

Glorified be the One who placed him, sallAllahu `alayhi wa sallam, in elevated and shining places and who carried him, sallAllahu `alayhi wa sallam, by night to "the distance of two bow's-length or nearer still." He supported him with uncountable miracles, equipped him with perfect qualities that are difficult to fully describe, gave him five favors that were never given to anyone before him, and gifted him with words which were concise but comprehensive.

In short, no one could achieve the Prophet's, sallAllahu `alayhi wa sallam, special status. For him, there is appropriate speech in every place; all perfection originates from his perfection.

He never puzzled at any question or response, and his tongue never spoke but the truth. What more can be said of the person who was described in the Holy Qur'an, and whose qualities were made known in all of the previous Holy Books.

Allah, Subhanahu wa Ta`ala, brought him to His Presence between His Vision and His Words and honored him by associating his name with His Own Name, to show and prove his high station. He made him the light and a blessing for the entire universe, and filled all hearts with happiness because of his birth!

Let me show you a place where mercy, kindness, compassion, aggression, repression, depression, happiness, anger, frustration, suppression all get submerged into love. Come away with me!

Let me show you how his essence and presence in this place brings tranquility, humility, endless possibility, sublimity, every victorious ability all submerged into one. Come away with me!

Let me show you how much he loves you and me more than love could ever be with horizons, without limit and mercy, without borders, a love that will set us free from all these endless boundaries. Come away with me!

Poem and artwork by Maliha Hashmi,
Madinah al-Munawarra, Saudi Arabia

Artwork by artist,
Doy Yuniarto Soewando,
Jakarta, Indonesia

DU'A, THE CLOSING PRAISE

All praise and thanks belong to Allah, Lord of all the worlds.
O Allah! Send Your blessings and peace upon our Beloved Prophet,
Sayyidina Muhammad, his family and all his companions.
AMEEN!

O Allah! Use our tongue to always praise and defend Your Prophet.
Make us to follow his way (sunnah) and to obey him,
and let us return to You loving him and his Community.
AMEEN!

O Allah! Please make us to enter the Garden
and its castles together with him!
AMEEN!

O Allah! Have mercy on us on the day
he intercedes for all creation to enter into Paradise.
AMEEN!

O Allah! Allow us to visit him in Madinatu 'l-Munawwara every year.
AMEEN!

O Allah! Make us to remember You
and remember him at every moment of our lives!
AMEEN!

O Allah! Clean us from our sins with the water of repentance
and cover our bad manners with the dress of forgiveness.
AMEEN!

O Allah! Last year there were brothers and sisters
amongst us who have returned to You.
RAHIMAHUMULLAAH,
have mercy on them!

Grant them the blessings and rewards of this gathering and its graces!
AMEEN!

O Allah! Please make us to always be thankful for Your Endless Favors
and to remember the Meeting with You.
AMEEN!

O Allah! Make us to listen and obey You.
We beg You, grant us the best of endings!
ALLAAHUMMA 'KFINAA SHARRAZH-ZHAALIMEEN,
our Lord, ward off from us the evil of tyrants! (3x)

O Allah! Keep us safe from the temptations of this worldly life.
AMEEN!

O Allah! Make this Noble Messenger our intercessor
and grant us for his sake a high station on Judgment Day.
AMEEN!

Artwork by
Rena Hasanli, 10
Baku, Azerbaijan

Artwork by
Sabira Hasanli, 11
Baku, Azerbaijan

O Allah! Grant us to drink from the Pond of Your Prophet Muhammad, sallAllahu `alayhi wa sallam, with an easy and unhurried drink, preventing us from thirsting ever again, and gather us under his Banner tomorrow.
AMEEN!

O Lord, for the sake of his high respect with You, forgive us, our fathers, our mothers, our teachers, and those to whom we are obliged, as well as those who arranged this blessed gathering on this day, all believers, men and women, all Muslims, men and women, the living as well as those who have passed on.
AMEEN!

Indeed, You are The Near, Answerer of all prayers,
WA QAADIYAL-HAAJAAT,
and granting all needs! (3x)
and You are The Forgiver of all sins and misdeeds,
YAA ARHAMAR-RAAHIMEEN,
O Most Merciful of the Merciful! (3x)

May Allah's Blessings be upon Muhammad, his Family and Companions and grant them peace. Glory to our Lord, the Lord of Honor and Power! He is free from what they ascribe to Him! And peace be upon the Messengers, and Praise be to the Lord of the worlds.
AMEEN! AL-FATIHAH!

أَعُوذُ بِاللهِ مِنَ الشَّيْطَانِ الرَّجِيمِ

بِسْمِ اللهِ الرَّحْمٰنِ الرَّحِيمِ ﴿١﴾ ٱلْحَمْدُ لِلّٰهِ رَبِّ الْعَالَمِينَ ﴿٢﴾ ٱلرَّحْمٰنِ الرَّحِيمِ ﴿٣﴾ مَالِكِ يَوْمِ الدِّينِ ﴿٤﴾ اِيَّاكَ نَعْبُدُ وَاِيَّاكَ نَسْتَعِينُ ﴿٥﴾ اِهْدِنَا الصِّرَاطَ الْمُسْتَقِيمَ ﴿٦﴾ صِرَاطَ الَّذِينَ آنْعَمْتَ عَلَيْهِمْ غَيْرِ الْمَغْضُوبِ عَلَيْهِمْ وَلَا الضَّالِّينَ ﴿٧﴾

1. Bismillaahir-Rahmaanir-Raheem
2. Alhamdulillaahi rabbil `alameen
3. Ar-rahmaanir-raheem
4. Maaliki yawmiddeen
5. Iyyaaka na`budu wa iyyaaka nasta`een
6. Ihdinas siraat al-mustaqeem
7. Siraat alladheena an`amta `alayhim ghayril maghdoobi `alayhim wa laddaalleen.

Ameen!

1. In the name of Allah, Most Gracious, Most Merciful.
2. Praise be to Allah, Lord of the Worlds,
3. Most Gracious, Most Merciful
4. Master of the Day of Judgment
5. It is You we worship and You we ask for help
6. Guide us to the Straight Path
7. The path of those upon whom You have bestowed favor, not of those who have earned Your anger or of those who are astray.

Ameen!

Surah al-Fatihah, 1:7

THE COMPLETE QASIDAH LYRICS

Artwork by Kovsar Gurban, 8
Baku, Azerbaijan

THE OPENING QASIDAH

O Lord, bestow blessings upon Muhammad.
O Lord, bestow blessings and peace upon him.

يَا رَبِّ صَلِّ عَلَى مُحَمَّد ۞ يَا رَبِّ صَلِّ عَلَيْهِ وَسَلِّمْ
Yaa Rabbi salli `alaa Muhammad
Yaa Rabbi salli `alayhi wa sallim

O Lord, bestow blessings upon Muhammad.
O Lord, grant him the station of interceding.

يَا رَبِّ صَلِّ عَلَى مُحَمَّد ۞ يَا رَبِّ بَلِّغْهُ الْوَسِيْلَة
Yaa Rabbi salli `alaa Muhammad
Yaa Rabbi balligh-hul-waseelah

O Lord, bestow blessings upon Muhammad.
O Lord, favor him above all the creations.

يَا رَبِّ صَلِّ عَلَى مُحَمَّد ۞ يَا رَبِّ خُصَّهُ بِالْفَضِيْلَة
Yaa Rabbi salli `alaa Muhammad
Yaa Rabbi khussahu bil-fadeelah

O Lord, bestow blessings upon Muhammad.
O Lord, be pleased with the companions.

يَا رَبِّ صَلِّ عَلَى مُحَمَّد ۞ يَا رَبِّ وَارْضَ عَنِ الصَّحَابَة
Yaa Rabbi salli `alaa Muhammad
Yaa Rabbi warda `anis-sahaabah

O Lord, bestow blessings upon Muhammad.
O Lord, be pleased with his descendants.

يَا رَبِّ صَلِّ عَلَى مُحَمَّد ۞ يَا رَبِّ وَارْضَ عَنِ السُّلَالَة
Yaa Rabbi salli `alaa Muhammad
Yaa Rabbi warda anis-sulaalah

O Lord, bestow blessings upon Muhammad.
O Lord, may You be pleased with the masters

يَا رَبِّ صَلِّ عَلَى مُحَمَّد ۞ يَا رَبِّ وَارْضَ عَنِ الْمَشَايِخ
Yaa Rabbi salli `alaa Muhammad
Yaa Rabbi warda `anil-mashaayikh

O Lord, bestow blessings upon Muhammad.
O Lord, may You have mercy on our parents.

يَا رَبِّ صَلِّ عَلَى مُحَمَّد ۞ يَا رَبِّ فَارْحَمْ وَالِدَيْنَا
Yaa Rabbi salli `alaa Muhammad
Yaa Rabbi Farham waalideena

O Lord, bestow blessings upon Muhammad.
O Lord, may You have mercy on all of us.

يَا رَبِّ صَلِّ عَلَى مُحَمَّد ۞ يَا رَبِّ وَارْحَمْنَا جَمِيْعاً
Yaa Rabbi salli `alaa Muhammad
Yaa Rabbi warhamnaa jamee`an

O Lord, bestow blessings upon Muhammad.
O Lord, may You have mercy on all Muslims.

يَا رَبِّ صَلِّ عَلَى مُحَمَّد ۞ يَا رَبِّ وَارْحَمْ كُلَّ مُسْلِم
Yaa Rabbi salli `alaa Muhammad
Yaa Rabbi warham kulla Muslim

O Lord, bestow blessings upon Muhammad.
O Lord, and forgive every sinner.

يَا رَبِّ صَلِّ عَلَى مُحَمَّد ۞ يَا رَبِّ وَاغْفِرْ لِكُلِّ مُذْنِب
Yaa Rabbi salli `alaa Muhammad
Yaa Rabbi waghfir li-kulli mudhnib

O Lord, bestow blessings upon Muhammad.
O Lord, O Hearer of our supplication!

يَا رَبِّ صَلِّ عَلَى مُحَمَّد ۞ يَا رَبِّ يَا سَامِعَ دُعَانَا
Yaa Rabbi salli `alaa Muhammad
Yaa Rabbi yaa saami` du`aanaa

يَا رَبِّ صَلِّ عَلَى مُحَمَّد ۞ يَا رَبِّ لَا تَقْطَعْ رَجَانَا Yaa Rabbi salli `alaa Muhammad Yaa Rabbi laa taqta` rajaanaa	O Lord, bestow blessings upon Muhammad. O Lord, may You not end our hopes.
يَا رَبِّ صَلِّ عَلَى مُحَمَّد ۞ يَا رَبِّ بَلِّغْنَا نَزُورُهْ Yaa Rabbi salli `alaa Muhammad Yaa Rabbi ballighnaa nazooruh	O Lord, bestow blessings upon Muhammad. O Lord, grant us to visit him at his resting place.
يَا رَبِّ صَلِّ عَلَى مُحَمَّد ۞ يَا رَبِّ تَغْشَانَا بِنُورِهْ Yaa Rabbi salli `alaa Muhammad Yaa Rabbi taghshaanaa bi noorih	O Lord, bestow blessings upon Muhammad. O Lord may You dress us with his light.
يَا رَبِّ صَلِّ عَلَى مُحَمَّد ۞ يَا رَبِّ حِفْظَانَكَ وَآمَانَكَ Yaa Rabbi salli `alaa Muhammad Yaa Rabbi hifzaanak wa amaanak	O Lord, bestow blessings upon Muhammad. O Lord, safeguard us with Your security.
يَا رَبِّ صَلِّ عَلَى مُحَمَّد ۞ يَا رَبِّ وَاسْكِنَّا جِنَانَكَ Yaa Rabbi salli `alaa Muhammad Yaa Rabbi waskinnaa jinaanak	O Lord, bestow blessings upon Muhammad. O Lord, may You let us reside in your Heavens.
يَا رَبِّ صَلِّ عَلَى مُحَمَّد ۞ يَا رَبِّ أَجِرْنَا مِنْ عَذَابِكَ Yaa Rabbi salli `alaa Muhammad Yaa Rabbi ajirnaa min `adhaabik	O Lord, bestow blessings upon Muhammad. O Lord, exclude us from Your punishment.
يَا رَبِّ صَلِّ عَلَى مُحَمَّد ۞ يَا رَبِّ وَارْزُقْنَا الشَّهَادَة Yaa Rabbi salli `alaa Muhammad Yaa Rabbi warzuqnaash-shahaadah	O Lord, bestow blessings upon Muhammad. O Lord, grant us with the station of the martyrs.
يَا رَبِّ صَلِّ عَلَى مُحَمَّد ۞ يَا رَبِّ حِطْنَا بِالسَّعَادَة Yaa Rabbi salli `alaa Muhammad Yaa Rabbi hitnaa bis-sa`aadah	O Lord, bestow blessings upon Muhammad. O Lord, may You envelop us with happiness.
يَا رَبِّ صَلِّ عَلَى مُحَمَّد ۞ يَا رَبِّ وَاصْلِحْ كُلَّ مُصْلِح Yaa Rabbi salli `alaa Muhammad Yaa Rabbi waslih kulla muslih	O Lord, bestow blessings upon Muhammad. O Lord, reform those who wish to change.
يَا رَبِّ صَلِّ عَلَى مُحَمَّد ۞ يَا رَبِّ وَاكْفِ كُلَّ مُؤْذِ Yaa Rabbi salli `alaa Muhammad Yaa Rabbi wakfee kulla mu'dhin	O Lord, bestow blessings upon Muhammad. O Lord, protect us from every harmful one.
يَا رَبِّ صَلِّ عَلَى مُحَمَّد ۞ يَا رَبِّ نَخْتِم بِالْمُشَفَّعْ Yaa Rabbi salli `alaa Muhammad Yaa Rabbi nakhtim bil-mushaffa`	O Lord, bestow blessings upon Muhammad. O Lord, we end with his name who intercedes.
يَا رَبِّ صَلِّ عَلَى مُحَمَّد ۞ يَا رَبِّ صَلِّ عَلَيْهِ وَسَلِّم Yaa Rabbi salli `alaa Muhammad Yaa Rabbi salli `alayhi wa sallim	O Lord, bestow blessings upon Muhammad; Bestow blessings upon him and grant him peace.

THE CARAVANER'S QASIDAH

صَلَاةُ اللّٰهِ مَا لَاحَتْ كَوَاكِبْ
عَلَى أَحْمَدْ خَيْرِ مَنْ رَكِبَ النَّجَائِبْ

SalaatuLlaahi maa laahat kawaakib
`Ala 'hmad khayri man rakiban-najaa'ib

Allah's Blessings appear as many as stars in the sky; upon Ahmad, the best of those who ride the camels.

حَدَى حَادِي السُّرَى بِاسْمِ الْحَبَائِبْ
فَهَزَّ الشُّكْرُ أَعْطَافَ الرَّكَائِبْ

Hadaa haadis-suraa bismil-habaa'ib
Fahazzas-sukru a`taafar-rakaa'ib

Swaying upon hearing the person who sang the name of the Beloved, touching emotions of those on the trail.

أَلَمْ تَرَهَا وَقَدْ مَدَّتْ خُطَاهَا
وَسَالَتْ مِنْ مَدَامِعِهَا سَحَائِبْ

Alam tarahaa wa qad maddat khutaahaa
wa saalat min madaami`iha sahaa'ib

Did you not see how it (the camel) took longer steps and tears poured from its eyes with joy?

وَمَالَتْ لِلْحِمَى طَرَباً وَحَنَّتْ
إِلَى تِلْكَ الْمَعَالِمِ وَالْمَلَاعِبْ

Wa maalat lil-himaa taraban wa hannat
Ila tilkal ma`aalami wal-malaa`ib

It turned towards those sites with aching heart, longing for its landmarks and playgrounds.

فَدَعْ جَذْبَ الزِّمَامِ وَلَا تَسُقْهَا
فَقَائِدُ شَوْقِهَا لِلْحَيِّ جَاذِبْ

Fada` jadhbaz-zimaami wa laa tasuqha
Fa qaa'idu shawqihaa lil-hayyi jaadhib

Don't hold on to the ropes, nor lead it; for the camel's longing for him will pull it to the Living One.

فَهِمْ طَرَباً كَمَا هَامَتْ وَإِلَّا
فَإِنَّكَ فِي طَرِيقِ الْحُبِّ كَاذِبْ

Fahim taraban kamaa haamat wa illaa
Fa innaka fee tareeqil-hubbi kaadhib

Be engulfed in happiness as was the camel, or else your love is insincere.

أَمَا هَذَا الْعَقِيقُ بَدَا وَهَذِى
قِبَابُ الْحَيِّ لَاحَتْ وَالْمَضَارِبْ

Amaa hadhal `aqeequ badaa wa haadhi
Qibaabul-hayya laahat wal-malaarib

There, the village al-Aqeeq, can be seen, the sight of village housetops and tents.

وَتِلْكَ الْقُبَّةُ الْخَضْرَا وَفِيهَا
نَبِيٌّ نُورُهُ يَجْلُو الْغَيَاهِبْ

wa tilkal-qubbatul-khadraa wa feehaa
Nabiyyun nooruhu yajlul-ghayaahib

And there is the Green Dome, within it a Prophet whose light brightens the darkness.

The blessings have been achieved, the meeting drew nigh, and happiness has arrived from every side.	وَقَدْ صَحَّ الرِّضَى وَدَنَا التَّلاَقِيْ وَقَدْ جَاءَ الْهَنَا مِنْ كُلِّ جَانِبْ	wa qad sahhar-ridaa wa danat-talaaqee wa qad jaa'al-hanaa min kulli jaanib
Say to yourselves not to waste time! Before us is the Beloved; today there is no obstruction.	فَقُلْ لِلنَّفْسِ دُوْنَكِ وَالتَّمَلِّيْ فَمَا دُوْنَ الْحَبِيْبِ الْيَوْمَ حَاجِبْ	Fa qul-lin nafsi doonaki wat-tamallee Famaa doonal-habeebil-yawma haajib
Be at ease when you are present with the Beloved, for happiness is achieved and not the contrary.	تَمَلَّيْ بِالْحَبِيْبِ بِكُلِّ قَصْدٍ فَقَدْ حَصَلَ الْهَنَا وَالصَّدُّ غَائِبْ	Tamallay bil-habeebi bi kulli qasdin Faqad hasalal-hanaa wad-diddu ghaa'ib
This is the Prophet, the Best of Creations, altogether of highest status and most honorable position.	نَبِيُّ اللهِ خَيْرُ الْخَلْقِ جَمْعاً لَهُ أَعْلَى الْمَنَاصِبِ وَالْمَرَاتِبْ	NabiyyuLlaahi khayrul-khalqi jam`aa Lahoo a`lal-manaasibi wal-maraatib
The Prophet who ranks high and is respected, receiving honor eternally as well as rank.	لَهُ الْجَاهُ الرَّفِيْعُ لَهُ الْمَعَالِيْ لَهُ الشَّرَفُ الْمُؤَبَّدُ وَالْمَنَاقِبْ	Lahul-jaahur-rafee`u lahul-ma`aalee lahush-sharaful-mu`abbadu wal-manaaqib
If every day we seek him, walking on our eyelashes, not on camels,	فَلَوْ أَنَّا سَعَيْنَا كُلَّ حِيْنٍ عَلَى الْأَحْدَاقِ لاَ فَوْقَ النَّجَائِبْ	Fa law annaa sa`aynaa kulla heenin alal-ahdaaqi laa fawqan-najaa'ib
and even if we celebrate the Mawlid every day as a reminder of Ahmad, truly it is a duty!	وَلَوْ أَنَّا عَمِلْنَا كُلَّ يَوْمٍ لِأَحْمَدَ مَوْلِداً قَدْ كَانَ وَاجِبْ	wa law annaa `amilnaa kulla yawmin Li Ahmada mawlidan qad kaana waajib
May blessings of Allah, The Protector, be upon him, as much as the shining lights of the stars,	عَلَيْهِ مِنَ الْمُهَيْمِنِ كُلَّ وَقْتٍ صَلاَةٌ مَا بَدَا نُوْرُ الْكَوَاكِبْ	Alayhi minal-muhaymini kulla waqtin Salaatun maa badaa noorul-kawaakib
that embraced all his Family and Companions, all of them, and also his goodly descendants.	تَعُمُّ الْآلَ وَالْأَصْحَابَ طُرّاً جَمِيْعَهُمْ وَعِتْرَتَهُ الْأَطَايِبْ	Ta`ummul aala wal-as-haaba turraan Jamee`ahumu wa `itratahul-ataayib

YAA NABI SALAAM 'ALAYKA

يَا نَبِي سَلامٌ عَلَيكَ ۞ يَا رَسُولُ سَلامٌ عَلَيكَ
يَا حَبِيبُ سَلامٌ عَلَيكَ ۞ صَلَوَاتُ اللّٰهِ عَلَيكَ

Yaa Nabee salaam `alayka
Yaa Rasool salaam `alayka
Yaa Habeeb salaam `alayka
salawaatuLlaah `alayka

O Prophet, peace be upon you!
O Messenger, peace be upon you!

O Beloved, peace be upon you!
Praises of Allah be upon you!

أَشْرَقَ الكَوْنُ ابْتِهَاجًا ۞ بِوُجُودِ الْمُصْطَفَىٰ أَحْمَدْ

Ashraqal-kawnub tihaajan
Bi wujoodil-mustafaa 'hmad

The world lit up shared brightly rejoicing with the birth of the Chosen One, Ahmad.

وَلِأَهْلِ الكَوْنِ أُنْسٌ ۞ وَسُرُورٌ قَدْ تَجَدَّدْ

wa li ahlil-kawni unsun
wa suroorun qad tajaddad

And members of the cosmos were at ease,
And happy with this renewal

فَاطْرَبُوا يَا اهْلَ الْمَثَانِي ۞ فَهَزَارُ الْيُمْنِ غَرَّدْ

Fatraboo ya 'h-lal mathaanee
Fa hazaarul-yumni gharrad

(The nightingale sings:) 'Be delighted, O settler of the two places with this good fortune."

وَاسْتَضِيئُوا بِجَمَالٍ ۞ فَاقَ فِي الْحُسْنِ تَفَرَّدْ

Wastadeeoo bi jamaalin
Faaqa fil-husni tafarrad

And seek the light from a beauty, that is exceedingly superior and unique.

وَلَنَا الْبُشْرَى بِسَعْدٍ ۞ مُسْتَمِرٍ لَيْسَ يَنْفَدْ

wa lanal-bushraa bi sa`din
Mustamirrin laysa yanfad

We received the good news, with continuous happiness never ending.

حَيْثُ أُوتِينَا عَطَاءً ۞ جَمَعَ الْفَخْرَ الْمُؤَبَّدْ

Haythu ooteenaa `ataa'an
Jama`al-fakhrul-mu'abbad

As we were given a gift, that encompassed eternal glory (for this life and the hereafter).

فَلِرَبِّي كُلُّ حَمْدٍ ۞ جَلَّ أَنْ يَحْصُرَهُ الْعَدْ

Fa li Rabbee kullu hamdin
Jalla an yahsurahul `ad

For my Lord all praises and,
thanks that are countless in number.

إِذْ حَبَانَا بِوُجُودِ ۞ الْمُصْطَفَى الْهَادِي مُحَمَّدْ

Idh habaanaa bi wujoodi
al-Mustafaal haadee Muhammad

Since He bestowed upon us the presence (birth) of Muhammad, the Chosen One and the Guide.

MARHABAN, MARHABAN

Greetings! Greetings! O the light of my eyes! Greetings! Greetings! O Grandfather of Husayn!	مَرْحَبًا مَرْحَبًا يَا نُوْرَ عَيْنِي ۞ مَرْحَبًا مَرْحَبًا جَدَّ الْحُسَيْنِ Marhaban, Marhaban yaa noora `aynee Marhaban, Marhaban jaddal-Husayni

Greetings! Prophet of Allah, welcome! For verily with you is our happiness!

مَرْحَبًا يَا رَسُوْلَ اللهِ أَهْلاً ۞ مَرْحَبًا بِكَ إِنَّا بِكَ نُسْعَدْ
Marhaban Yaa Rasoolullaahi ahlan
Marhaban bika innaa bika nus`ad

Greetings! With his high rank, O our Lord, Greetings! Give generously and fulfill all our intentions

مَرْحَبًا وَبِجَاهِهْ يَا إِلَهِي ۞ مَرْحَبًا جُدْ وَبَلِّغْ كُلَّ مَقْصَدْ
Marhaban wa bi jaahih yaa ilaahi
Marhaban jud wa balligh kulla maqsad

Greetings! Guide us with his methods and directions. Greetings! So that we receive happiness and guidance.

مَرْحَبًا وَاهْدِنَا نَهْجَ سَبِيْلِهْ ۞ مَرْحَبًا كَيْ بِهِ نُسْعَدْ وَنُرْشَدْ
Marhaban wahdinaa nahja sabeelih
Marhaban kay bihi nus`ad wa nurshad

RABEE FAGHFIRLEE

O my Lord! Forgive me, for I have sins, O Allah, with blessings of my guide Muhammad, O Allah!	رَبِّ فَاغْفِرْ لِي ذُنُوْبِي يَا الله ۞ بِبَرَكَةِ الْهَادِي مُحَمَّدْ يَا الله Rabbi faghfir lee dhunoobee, yaa Allah Bi-barakatil-haadee Muhammad, yaa Allah

O my Lord, let us reach (our goal) for the sake of his high rank (with You). In his proximity is the best place to stay, O Allah!

رَبِّ بَلِّغْنَا بِجَاهِهْ يَا الله ۞ فِي جِوَارِهْ خَيْرَ مَقْعَدْ يَا الله
Rabbi ballighnaa bi jaahih, yaa Allah
fee jiwaarih khayra maq`ad, yaa Allah

May Allah's Blessings shower him, O Allah! O Noblest of Messengers, Muhammad, O Allah!

وَصَلاةُ اللهِ تَغْشَى يَا الله ۞ أَشْرَفَ الرُّسْلِ مُحَمَّدْ يَا الله
wa salaatuLlaahi taghshaa, yaa Allah
ashrafar-rusli Muhammad, ya Allah

Peace be upon him without end, O Allah, renewed with every moment, O Allah!

وَسَلامٌ مُسْتَمِرٌّ يَا الله ۞ كُلَّ حِيْنٍ يَتَجَدَّدْ يَا الله
wa salaamun mustamirrun, yaa Allah
kulla heenin yatajaddad, yaa Allah

TALA'AL BADRU 'ALAYNA

O the full moon rose above us
From the valley of wadaa`a.

Gratitude is our obligation
as long as any caller calls to Allah.

ظَلَعَ الْبَدْرُ عَلَيْنَا ۞ مِنْ ثَنِيَّاتِ الْوَدَاعْ
وَجَبَ الشُّكْرُ عَلَيْنَا ۞ مَا دَعَا لِلَّهِ دَاعْ
Tala`al badru `alayna, min thaneeyatil-wadaa`a
Wajabash-shukru `alayna, maa da`aaliLlaahi daa`i

O you who were sent among us!
You came with the orders to be obeyed.

أَيُّهَا الْمَبْعُوثُ فِينَا ۞ جِئْتَ بِالْأَمْرِ الْمُطَاعْ
Ayyuhal mab`ootho feena, Ji'ta bil-amril-mutaa`a

Be our intercessor, O our Beloved,
on the Day of Collection and Gathering!

كُنْ شَفِيعًا يَا حَبِيبِي ۞ يَوْمَ حَشْرٍ وَاجْتِمَاعْ
Kun shafi`an yaa habibi, Yawma hashrin wajtimaa`a

O our Lord! Send Your Blessings on the one,
who appeared in the best of all places.

رَبَّنَا صَلِّ عَلَى مَنْ ۞ حَلَّ فِي خَيْرِ الْبِقَاعْ
Rabbanaa salli `alaa man, halla fee khayril-biqaa`a

You are the savior of us all,
O You who gathers all perfected character traits!

أَنْتَ غَوْثُنَا جَمِيعًا ۞ يَا مُجَمَّلَ الطِّبَاعْ
Anta ghawthunaa jamee`an, Yaa mujammalat tibaa`a

We were adorned with the robe of honor,
after patches and tatters

وَلَبِسْنَا ثَوْبَ عِزٍّ ۞ بَعْدَ تَلْفِيقِ الرِّقَاعْ
Wa labisnaa thawba `izzin, Ba`da talfeeqir-riqaa`a

Cover up our shortcomings,
O Answerer of all requests!

أَسْبِلِ السِّتْرَ عَلَيْنَا ۞ يَا مُجِيبًا كُلَّ دَاعِي
Asbilis-sitra `alaynaa, Yaa mujeeban kulla daa`i

And Allah's blessing be upon Ahmad,
on the numbers of the freed lands.

وَصَلَاةُ اللهِ عَلَى أَحْمَدْ ۞ عَدَّ تَحْرِيرِ الرِّقَاعِ
Wa salaatuLlaah `alaa Ahmad, `adda tahreerir-riqaa`i

And likewise, the Family and the Companions,
as long as the striving is for Allah.

وَكَذَا آلٍ وَصَحْبٍ ۞ مَا سَعَى لِلَّهِ سَاعْ
Wa kadhaa aalin wa sahbin, Maa sa`aa liLlaahi saa`a

SALLALLAHU 'ALA MUHAMMAD

Allah's Salutations be upon Muhammad!
Allah's Salutations be upon him
with abundant peace!

صَلَّى اللهُ عَلَى مُحَمَّدْ ۞ صَلَّى اللهُ عَلَيْهِ وَسَلَّمْ
SallAllahu `ala Muhammad, SallAllahu `alayhi wa sallam

O my Lord, make our gathering's
purpose a good ending.

رَبِّ وَاجْعَلْ مُجْتَمَعْنَا ۞ غَايَتُهُ حُسْنُ الْخِتَامِ
Rabbi waj`al mujtama`na, ghayat-hu husnul-khitaami

And grant us what we are asking,
from Your great favors.

وَأَعْطِنَا مَا قَدْ سَأَلْنَا ۞ مِنْ عَطَايَاكَ الْجِسَامِ
Wa `tinaa maa qad sa'alna, min `ataayakal-jisaami

And bless the souls among us,
a meeting with the Best of Created Beings.

وَاكْرِمِ الْأَرْوَاحَ مِنَّا ۞ بِلِقَى خَيْرِ الْأَنَامِ
Wakrimil-irwaaha minna, bi liqaa khayril-anaami

And convey to the Chosen One, from us,
Blessings and Greetings of Peace.

وَابْلِغِ الْمُخْتَارَ عَنَّا ۞ مِنْ صَلَاةٍ وَسَلَامْ
Wablighil-mukhtaaru `anna, min salaatin wa salaami

O Allah, O Muhammad,
O Abu Bakr as-Siddiq!

يَا اللهُ يَا مُحَمَّدْ ۞ يَا أَبَا بَكْرٍ يَا صِدِّيقْ
Yaa Allahu Yaa Muhammad, Yaa Aba Bakr Yaa Siddeeq

O Umar, Uthman, O Ali,
Fatimah, daughter of the Prophet!

يَا عُمَرْ عُثْمَانْ يَا عَلِي ۞ فَاطِمَةَ بِنْتَ رَسُولِ
Yaa `Umar, `Uthmaan, Yaa `Ali, Fatimah binta Rasooli

QASIDAH BURDA

يَا رَبِّ بِالْمُصْطَفَى بَلِّغْ مَقَاصِدَنَا
وَاغْفِرْ لَنَا مَا مَضَى يَا وَاسِعَ الْكَرَمِ

Yaa Rabbee bil-Mustafaa balligh maqaasidanaa
Waghfir lanaa maa madaa yaa waasi`al-karami

O my Lord! By means of the Chosen One, let us achieve our goals.
And forgive our past (misdeeds), O Possessor of Vast Generosity!

يَا أَكْرَمَ الْخَلْقِ مَا لِي مَنْ أَلُوذُ بِهِ
سِوَاكَ عِنْدَ حُلُولِ الْحَادِثِ الْعَمِمِ

Yaa akramal-khalqi maa lee man aloodhu bihi
Siwaaka `inda huloolil haadithil `amimi

Most Generous of Mankind, I have no one to take refuge in except you at occurrence of widespread calamity.

وَلَنْ يَضِيقَ رَسُولَ اللَّهِ جَاهُكَ بِي
إِذَا الْكَرِيمُ تَجَلَّى بِاسْمِ مُنْتَقِمِ

wa lan yadeeqa rasoollullahi jaahuka bee
Idhal-kareemu tajallee bismi muntaqimi

And O Messenger of Allah, your exalted status will not diminish from your intercession for me when The Most Bountiful manifests with the Name of Avenger.

فَإِنَّ مِنْ جُودِكَ الدُّنْيَا وَضَرَّتَهَا
وَمِنْ عُلُومِكَ عِلْمَ اللَّوْحِ وَالْقَلَمِ

Fa inna min joodikad-dunya wa darratahaa
wa min `uloomika `ilmal-lawhi wal-qalami

Verily, amongst your bounties is this world and the Next, and of your knowledge is knowledge of the Preserved Tablets and the Pen.

يَا نَفْسُ لَا تَقْنَطِي مِنْ زَلَّةٍ عَظُمَتْ
إِنَّ الْكَبَائِرَ فِي الْغُفْرَانِ كَاللَّمَمِ

Yaa nafsu laa taqnatee min zallatin `adhumat
Innal-kabaa'ira fil-ghufraani kal-lamami

O my self! Do not despair due to your grave sins. Even the greatest sins when pardoned are minor.

لَعَلَّ رَحْمَةَ رَبِّي حِينَ يَقْسِمُهَا
تَأْتِي عَلَى حَسَبِ الْعِصْيَانِ فِي الْقِسَمِ

La`alla rahmata Rabbee heena yaqsimuhaa
Ta'tee `alaa hasabil `isyaani fil-qisami

Perhaps the mercy of my Lord when divided up, would be distributed in proportion to the sins.

يَا رَبِّ وَاجْعَلْ رَجَائِي غَيْرَ مُنْعَكِسٍ
لَدَيْكَ وَاجْعَلْ حِسَابِي غَيْرَ مُنْخَرِمِ

Yaa Rabbi waj`al rajaa'i ghayra mun`akisin
Ladayka waj`al hisaabee ghayra munkharimi

O my Lord! Let not my hopes be rejected by You, And let not my reckoning reveal my deficiencies.

وَالْطُفْ بِعَبْدِكَ فِي الدَّارَيْنِ إِنَّ لَهُ
صَبْرًا مَتَى تَدْعُهُ الْأَهْوَالُ يَنْهَزِمِ

wal-tuf bi `abdika fid-daarayni inna lahu
Sabran mataa tad`uhul-ahwaalu yanhazimi

Be kind to Your servant in both the worlds, for verily his patience, when called upon by hardships, runs away.

وَائْذَنْ لِسُحْبِ صَلَاةٍ مِنْكَ دَائِمَةٍ
عَلَى النَّبِيِّ بِمُنْهَلٍّ وَمُنْسَجِمِ

wa' dhan li-suhbi salaatin minka daa'imatin
a`lan nabiyyi bi munhallin wa munsajimi

So order clouds of blessings from You perpetually Upon the Prophet abundantly and gently.

وَالْآلِ وَالصَّحْبِ ثُمَّ التَّابِعِينَ
فَهُمْ أَهْلُ التُّقَى وَالنُّقَى وَالْحِلْمِ وَالْكَرَمِ

wal-aali was-sahbi thummat-taabi`eena
Fahum ahlut-tuqaa wan-nuqaa wal-hilmi wal-karami

And upon his family his Sahabah, then upon those who follow them, the people of piety, knowledge, clemency and generosity.

'ALAL-MADINAH

عَلَى الْمَدِينَةْ عَلَى الْمَدِينَةْ ❁ رَبِّ بَلِّغْنَا زِيَارَةْ نَبِيْنَا

`Alal-Madinah, `alal-Madinah
Rabbi ballighnaa ziyaarat nabeenaa

To Madinah, onwards to Madinah!
My Lord, grant us a visit to our Prophet!

رَبِّ بَلِّغْنَا نَزُورُ الْحَضْرَةْ ❁ وَنُشَاهِدْ آحْمَدْ وَالْقُبَّةْ الْخَضْرَا
نَهْتِفْ جَمِيعاً يَا أَبَا الزَّهْرَةْ ❁ نَحْنُ زُوَّارَكْ فَكُنْ ضَمِيناً

Rabbi ballighnaa nazoorul-hadrah,
wan-shaahid Ahmad wal-qubbal-khadraa
Nahtif jamee`an yaa Abaz-Zahrah
nahnu zuwwaarak fakun dameenaa

My Lord, grant us to visit the living one,
to witness Ahmad and the Green Dome.
So we all cry out: "O Father of Zahra,
we are your guests, so give us your Guarantee!"

رَبِّ بَلِّغْنَا زِيَارَةْ طَهَ ❁ وَنْشُوفَ الرَّوْضَةْ وَنْصَلِّي حَدَاهَا
وَنْقُولْ يَا نَبِي يَا عَظِيمَ الْجَاهْ ❁ كُنْ لِي مُجِيراً كُنْ لِي مُعِيناً

Rabbi ballighnaa ziyaarat Taahaa
wan-shoofir-rawda wan-sallee hadaahaa
wanqool yaa Nabee yaa `azheemaal jaah
kun lee mujeeran kun lee mu`eenaa

My Lord, grant us to visit Taha,
to see Paradise's Garden and pray in it,
and to say, "O Prophet of high esteem,
be my neighbor, be my aid!"

قَصْدِي إِلَى نَحْوِكُمْ أَسِيرُ ❁ وَالدَّمْعُ مِنْ مُقْلَتِي غَزِيرُ
وَالْقَلْبُ فِي حُبِّكُمْ أَسِيرُ ❁ يَا قَلْبِي اِفْرَحْ هَذَا نَبِيْنَا

Qasdee ilaa nahwikum aseeru
wad-dam`u min muqlatee ghazeeru
wal-qalboo fee hubbikum aseeru
yaa qalbee ifrah hadhaa Nabeenaa

My firm intention and my steps are but to reach
you, while from my eyes flow tears without cease.
My heart is a hostage to your love,
while my heart rejoices, "this is our Prophet!"

سَاقِي الْحُمَيَّا عَرِّجْ عَلَيّ ❁ وَاسْقِنِي هَيَّا كَأْساً وَفِيَّا
وَامْدَحْ مُحَمَّدْ خَيْرَ الْبَرِيَّةْ ❁ فَهُوَ الشَّفِيعُ لِلْمُذْنِبِينْ

Saaqil humayyah `arrij `alayya
was-qinee hayyaa ka'san wafeeyaa
wamdah Muhammad khayral-bareeyya
fa-huwash-shafee`u lil-mudhnibeena

Cupbearer of the attendees, tend me,
and pour me a full cup to drink,
praise Muhammad, the Best of Creation;
he is the Intercessor of all sinners

NAHRAN MIN LABAN

إِنَّ فِي الْجَنَّةِ نَهْرًا مِنْ لَبَنْ ۞ لِعَلِيٍّ وَحُسَيْنٍ وَحَسَنْ

Inna fil-jannati nahran min laban
li `Aliyyin wa Husaynin wa Hasan

In Heaven there is a river of milk
for Ali and Husayn and Hasan

يَا رَسُولاً قَدْ حَبَانَا حُبُّهُ فَضْلاً وَمَنْ
جُدْ عَلَيْنَا بِالتَّجَلِّي نَرْتَجِي مِنْكَ الْمِنَنْ

Yaa Rasoolan qad habaanaa
hubbuhu fadlan wa man
Jud `alaynaa bit-tajallee
nartajee minkal-minan

O Messenger, whose love
has rewarded us with favors and grants!
Be generous to us with your manifestation,
we seek from you all favors.

جِئْتُ شَوْقًا وَغَرَامًا فِي هَوَى قَلْبِي حَسَنْ
رَاجِيًا مِنْهُ ابْتِسَامًا مَنْ لَهُ رُوحِي ثَمَنْ

Ji'tu shawqan wa gharaaman
fee hawaa qalbee Hasan
raajiyan minhub tisaaman
man lahur-roohee thaman

I came full of love and yearning
and my heart full with desire,
hoping a smile from him for whom
my soul is the price.

مِنْ فُؤَادِي وَحَنِينِي وَحَنِينٌ قَلْبِي وَعَنْ
وَرَأَى الطَّيْرُ حَنِينِي تَبْكِي عَطْفًا وَعَنْ

Min fu'aadee wa haneenee
wa haneen qalbee wa `an
wa ra'aat-tayru haneenee
tabkee `atfaan wa `an

From my heart, my yearning,
the longing of my heart and its sighs,
the birds saw my longing
and in sympathy joined in.

وَصَلَاتِي وَسَلَامِي لِلنَّبِيِّ الْمُؤْتَمَنْ
رَاجِيًا حُسْنَ الْخِتَامِ بِالْحُسَيْنِ وَالْحَسَنْ

wa salaatee wa salaamee
lin-Nabiyyil mu'taman
raajiyan husnal-khitaami
bil Husayni wal Hasan

My praise and greetings
upon the trusted Prophet
Hoping a good end by means of
al-Husayn and al-Hasan!

A TEST OF LOVE
How Well Do You Know Your Prophet?
sallAllahu `alayhi wa sallam

Artwork by artist,
Alice Skachkova
Moscow, Russia

Check your answers on the next page and add up your points. Remember not to look at the answers until you finish!

1. What is Mawlid an-Nabi? (5 points)
2. When and where was our Prophet ﷺ born? What year is that known as? (20 points)
3. What is the name of our Prophet's ﷺ mother? (5 points)
4. What is the name of our Prophet's ﷺ father? (5 points)
5. When did our Prophet's ﷺ parents pass away? (10 points)
6. Where did our Prophet ﷺ receive the first revelation and how old was he? (5 points)
7. Where is our Beloved Prophet's ﷺ holy resting place? (5 points)
8. What is the name of the Prophet's ﷺ wetnurse? (5 points)
9. Who took care of our Prophet ﷺ after his mother died? (10 points)
10. List the names of our Prophet's ﷺ children. (35 points)
11. Name the lineage of the Prophet ﷺ up to 'Hashim'. (20 points)
12. Mention one extraordinary event that took place when he ﷺ was born. (10 points)
13. List at least five miracles of our Prophet ﷺ including the most important and long lasting one. (25 points)
14. Mention one great benefit of the Mawlid, in other words, celebrating the Birth of our Beloved Prophet ﷺ. (100 points)
15. Name at least five rewardable deeds done during the Mawlid. (50 points)
16. Name at least three Asma an-Nabi, names of our Beloved Prophet ﷺ. (3 points)

BONUS #1: There is a poem or Qasidah that is one of the most widely recited and memorised poems in the world. It was written in the 7th century Hijri by someone deeply in love with the Prophet ﷺ. He composed this poem after becoming paralyzed from a stroke as a means of seeking Allah's forgiveness and the Prophet's intercession. One night, in his dream, he saw himself reciting the Qasidah to the Holy Prophet ﷺ who then touched the paralyzed part of his body and placed his holy cloak or Burdah over him. On awakening, he discovered he had been cured of his illness! What is the name of this Qasidah? (MULTIPLY your total with 1,000 points!)

BONUS #2: What is the name of an important salawat book that lovers of the Prophet ﷺ from around the world have been reciting daily for hundreds and thousands of years?

Hint: The title consists of two words. The second word is written in Arabic as: الْخَيْرَات

(MULTIPLY your total with 1,000,000 points!)

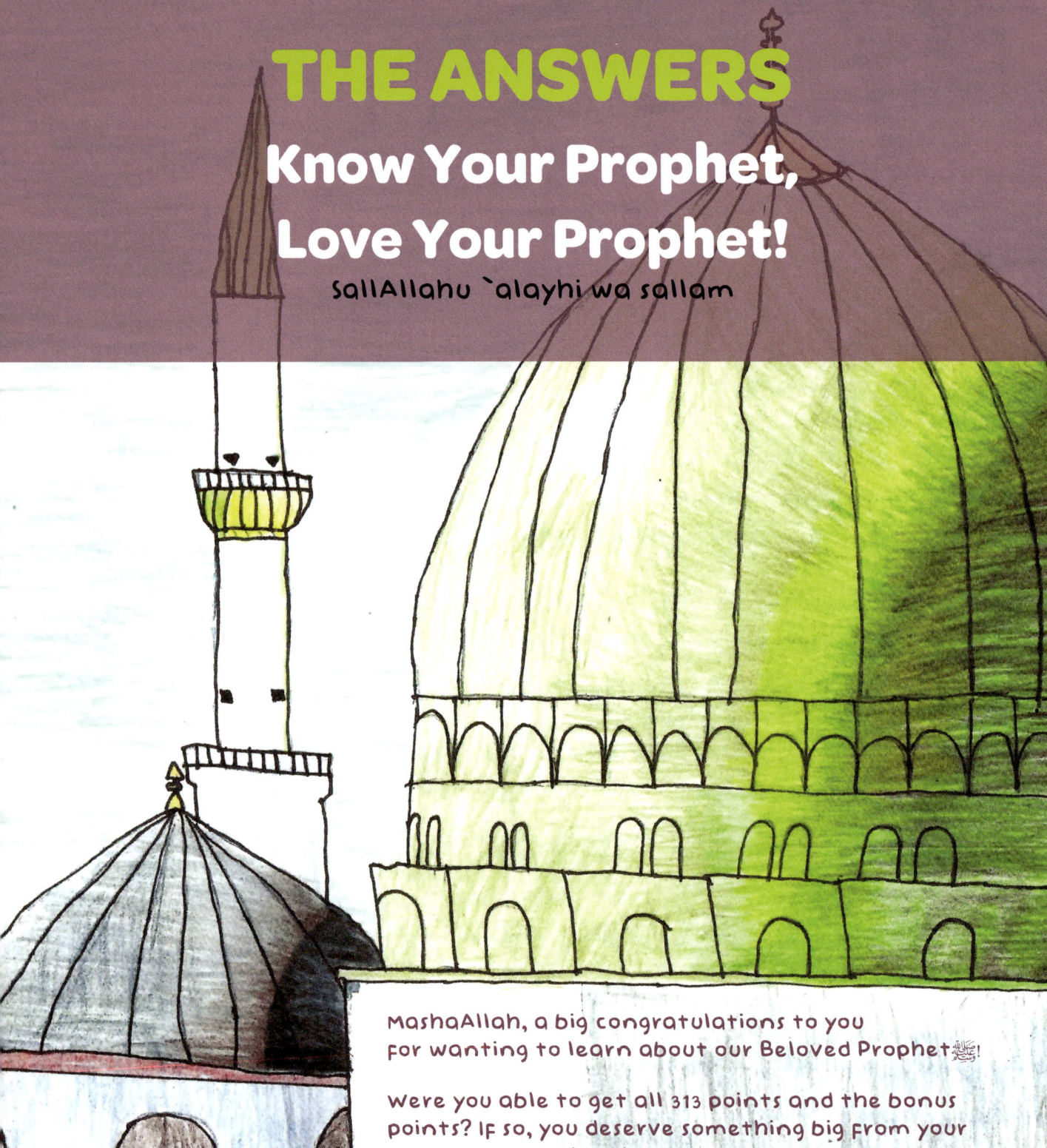

THE ANSWERS
Know Your Prophet, Love Your Prophet!
sallAllahu `alayhi wa sallam

Artwork by Fatima, 11 Maryland, USA

MashaAllah, a big congratulations to you for wanting to learn about our Beloved Prophet ﷺ!

Were you able to get all 313 points and the bonus points? If so, you deserve something big from your parents or teachers!

And may Allah and His Beloved ﷺ reward you with something greater and bigger, inshaallah!

1. Mawlid an-Nabi, Arabic for the "birthday of the Prophet", is the celebration of the birth of our Beloved Prophet Muhammad ﷺ.

2. Prophet Muhammad ﷺ was born in Makkah al-Mukarrama in a place called "Suq ul-Layl". He was born on a Monday, on the 12th day of the month of Rabi'ul Awwal, in the year 571 of the western calendar. At that time, the people named years by major events. He was born in the year known as the "Year of the Elephant" when Abraha, the Abyssinian, marched an army to Mecca, intending to destroy the Ka`bah. The army was led by a war elephant named Mahmud. When the army arrived at the gates of Mecca, Mahmud stopped and refused to enter. That is when Allah destroyed Abraha and his army by sending flocks of birds named Ababil that dropped small stones on them. Fifty days later, in this Year of the Elephant, our Beloved Prophet ﷺ was born.

3. The name of the Prophet's mother is Aminah Bint Wahb.

4. The name of the Prophet's father is `Abdullah Ibn `Abdul-Muttalib.

5. The Prophet's father, `Abdullah, died while Aminah was still pregnant with the Prophet. He did not get the opportunity to see The Best and The Last of All Prophets. He died when Aminah was six months pregnant with the Prophet. Aminah Bint Wahb, the Prophet's mother, died when the Prophet was only six years old.

6. The Prophet ﷺ received the first wahiyy, revelation of Prophethood, in the Cave of Hira near Mecca when he was 40 years old.

7. The Prophet ﷺ passed away in Madinah al-Munawwara and was buried therein.

8. Her name is Halimah as-Sa'diyyah. It was the habit of Arab women to breastfeed other than their own children. Halimah raised the Prophet until he was two years and two months old, after which she returned him to his mother.

9. The Prophet's ﷺ mother died when he was six years old. The Prophet was then raised by his grandfather `Abdul-Muttalib. When the Prophet's mother died, his grandfather hugged him and showed feelings towards the Prophet that he never showed towards his own son. When `Abdul Muttalib was dying, he asked the Prophet's uncle Abu Talib to take care of the Prophet ﷺ.

10. The Prophet ﷺ had seven children, all of whom passed away during his lifetime except for his daughter, Fatimatuz-Zahra, who passed away six months after the Prophet's passing. The names of his seven children are: Al-Qasim, `Abdullah, Zaynab, Ruqayyah, Ummu Kulthum, Fatima and Ibrahim.

11. He is Muhammad, the son of `Abdullah, the son of `Abdul-Muttalib, the son of Hashim, from the tribe of Quraysh.

12. A star was born the night he was born, known as the "The Star of Ahmad"; a light came out with him, illuminating what is between the East and West; the enourmous fire of the fire worhippers in Persia which had been burning for thousands of years died out and its palaces collapsed; the idols inside the Ka`bah broke and fell down; all devils and jinn of the sky were pelted by burning meteors.

13. The number of the Prophet's miracles reached 3000 in his lifetime; the most important is The Holy Qur'an. Other miracles include: crying of the tree trunk; the camel speaking and seeking refuge in him; the speaking of the wolf and his testimony; the water coming out from between his fingers; returning the eye of the Prophet's Companion, Sayyidina Qatadah ibn al-Nu'man; Mount Uhud wanting to turn itself into gold for the Prophet; the testification of the tree; splitting of the moon; the Night of Israa and Mi'raaj, etc.

14. Mawlid an-Nabi inspires the heart to have a more profound love for our Prophet ﷺ.

15. Muslims all over the world join together to do rewardable deeds during the Mawlid celebration, such as: reciting the Holy Qur'an; reciting lots of salawat; chanting Islamic songs that praise the Prophet; narrating stories about the Prophet's birth and his life; speaking about his physical description and his great manners; organizing fun activities for young children to make them happy with their Prophet; feeding the poor, decorating the homes, mosque and streets and handing out sweets to neighbors out of love for the Prophet ﷺ, etc.

16. Prophet Muhammad ﷺ has 201 blessed names, as listed by Imam al-Jazuli. Some of these names are: Muhammad, Ahmad, Hamid, Mahmud, Mustafa, Taha, Yaseen, al-Mahi, al-Hashir, al-Aqib.

BONUS #1: The poem is Qasidah al-Burdah, Poem of the Blessed Cloak, written by Imam al-Busayri.
BONUS #2: The salawat book is Dala'il al-Khayrat, compiled by Imam Sulayman al-Jazuli.

SIMPLE SUNNAHS, BIG REWARDS

How many of Prophet Muhammad's ﷺ sunnahs can you follow daily? Make a sunnah chart like the one below with different sunnahs that you can follow. Then hang it in your room as a reminder!

Keep Smiling!	Greet each other with "As-salamu 'alaykum!"	Give gifts to one another	Speak good or remain silent
Feed the hungry and help the needy	Listen to the Adhan and reply to it	Read or listen to the Holy Qur'an	Speak the truth and keep your promises
Pray at night while people are asleep	Say "Alhamdulillah" after sneezing	Take care of your hair by combing it	Visit relatives and friends
Bathe and cut nails on the day of Jumu'ah	Wear white clothes and put on nice smell on Jumu'ah	Increase Salawat upon the Prophet ﷺ on Fridays	Show love and kindness to your parents
Wash hands before and after eating	Sit down while eating and drinking	Say "Bismillahi 'r-Rahmani 'r-Rahim" before every meal	Break your fast with dates or water
Begin and end your meal with salt	Drink water in three sips	Take an afternoon nap after dhuhr prayer	Brush your teeth with the miswak
Put shoes on starting with the right foot and take them off starting with the left foot	Recite Surah al-Ikhlaas, al-Falaq, an-Naas three times and one Ayat al-Kursi before sleeping	Make wudu before sleeping at night	Sleep on your right side, facing the Qibla

LET'S FOLLOW HIS FOOTSTEPS!

Follow the footsteps of our Beloved Prophet ﷺ by following his sunnahs! Each Holy Sandal in this maze represents a sunnah of our Prophet. Every time you follow a sunnah, color in a Holy Sandal until you reach your destination!

Allah is telling His Beloved Prophet in the Holy Qur'an:

(O Muhammad!) Say to them:
"IF YOU REALLY LOVE ALLAH, THEN FOLLOW ME!
Allah will love you and forgive your sins,
and Allah is Oft-Forgiving, Most Merciful."
(Surah 'Aali Imraan, 3:31)

اللّٰهُ

What are some of the sunnahs these two dervishes are following? There are at least nine!

MAWLID AN-NABI ﷺ MUBARAK!

COME! LET US CELEBRATE THE BIRTH AND LIFE OF OUR BELOVED PROPHET, SAYYIDINA MUHAMMAD, sallAllahu `alayhi wa sallam, today, tomorrow and EVERY DAY!

Artwork by artist Amir al-Zubi, Bosnia and Herzegovina